WANDERLUST WARRIOR
P R O J E C T

*Discover You. With Us.*

MICHELLE ROSE GILMAN
PETER MIKULECKY, PH.D.
WITH REBEKAH TAYEBI, MSW

Printed in Canada

First Printing, 2019

ISBN-13: 978-1-941768-47-1 print edition
ISBN-13: 978-1-941768-48-8 ebook edition
ISBN-13: 978-1-941768-49-5 audio edition

**Waterside Productions**
2055 Oxford Ave
Cardiff, CA 92007
www.waterside.com

*For Noah. For Everything.*
MICHELLE ROSE GILMAN

*For all my salty, swashbuckling teachers.*
*And for my stunning hobbit.*
PETER MIKULECKY

*Who else, but for Sarah.*
REBEKAH TAYEBI

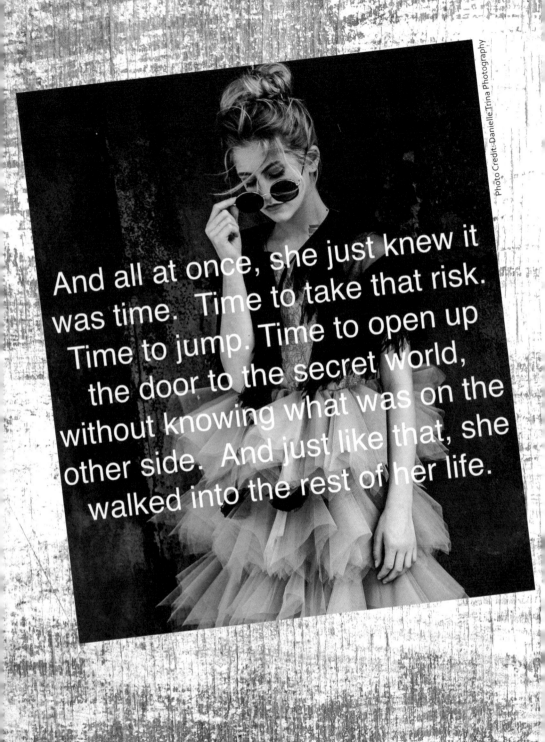

And all at once, she just knew it was time. Time to take that risk. Time to jump. Time to open up the door to the secret world, without knowing what was on the other side. And just like that, she walked into the rest of her life.

# WHAT'S OUR MISSION?

The Wanderlust Warrior Project is a community that encourages authentic-

ity and strength in young women ages 13-23. The movement challenges the

myriad forces, both cynical and well-intentioned, that conspire to quell cu-

riosity and individuality among members of our tribe. By creating space for

each of us to ask our own questions, the movement empowers women to

follow their own path in life. The movement fosters courage, wisdom and a

relentless passion for truth.

# ACKNOWLEDGEMENTS

The authors would like to thank our focus group of Brand Advisors: Julia Cathey, Alyssa Grace Dilorio, Lauren Reveley, and Avonley Kliewer; you girls were instrumental in the early stages of this book.

Special thanks to Bill Gladstone, our literary agent for over 20 years, and to Waterside Publishing for believing in our project. A creative artist's nod to Ken Fraser, for the artwork on the beautiful cover, and to Christy Salinas for her creative work on the interior of the book. Thanks to Nichole Panik Earle, from The Lanyap Group, who did early work on some of the graphics and brought the Walkabouts to life. We owe a debt to the eyes of our two photographers, Danielle Trina Photography and Noah Gilman Photography. You nailed the vision. And to all the inspiring women who agreed to be interviewed for this book, thank you for caring about our tribe, and sharing your most heartfelt words. Most importantly, we want to thank all of our students over the last 30 years, who have taught us what they needed to thrive, and how and who they wanted to be. We honor you and we see you.

# TABLE OF CONTENTS

# INTRODUCTION

*Hello!*

We're so glad you picked up this book! If you're reading this, there is a reason. Perhaps the title made you curious. Or maybe this book was given to you as a gift. However it found you, we know it's in good hands—yours!

This book begged to be written. Our collective decades of experience as educators and entrepreneurs working with young women made that clear. But, really, we wouldn't have needed all that experience to see the need. We'd simply need to have paid attention to what was going on around us. When we first decided to embark on this adventure, we researched other books written for you, the young woman. What we found disappointed and embarrassed us. Most of the books written for you were filled with chapters like, "How to make the best weight loss smoothie," along with some inspirational words, and then another chapter such as, "How to get your body ready for the beach," followed by some motivational pages on "Living your best life." While we realize that there is a market for those types of books, there didn't seem to be any *smart* books written for you, ones that offered more substantial, thoughtful advice. We believe that the reason for the scarcity is that authors felt they couldn't hold your attention without including that silliness. But we know YOU. We know what you yearn for, what you are asking, what you want to know about a life well-lived. We are speaking directly to your heart, your soul, your mind and that special part of you that already knows that conforming, being like everybody else, is not your path.

So, right up front, WE ARE NOT INCLUDING smoothie recipes, tips for picking out the best sunglasses for your face shape, and the like. If you want to read about "tightening your abs" or "updating your Spring wardrobe to increase your self-esteem," put down this book right now. It's not for you. This book is not a cheerleading book. It is not a book with cute little catch phrases to make you feel happy. We're not here to fix you, change you, make you prettier, or fill you up with bogus and superficial anecdotes about success.

This book is about becoming a strong woman in the world. It will ask you hard questions about independence and connection. About honesty and doubt. About strength and compassion. Rather than try to smooth your edges, this book will encourage you to embrace the "all" of you. All the messy, beautiful, quirky, joyful, painful, bewildering, loving parts that make you, you! It's not a book to help you fit in or conform to the crowd. It's a book about thinking for yourself, and rejecting all the lies that you have been told about how to live, how to behave, what your life should be about, how to define success and what you *should* be feeling, doing and acting as a woman in the world.

Because yes, you have been told lies. These lies might have come in the form of well-intentioned advice from trusted loved ones—all parents want the best for their child. Teachers do, too! Although we call some of their guidance lies, they offer it to you out of love. We're not throwing shade on those who love you. Promise. However, there are other sources that lie without such loving intentions. Social media doesn't love you. It loves itself. It stuffs your mind with untruths and unattainable goals (don't get us wrong—we've been known to waste countless, mindless hours online too—we get ya!). Other lies are simply made-up, society rules about how your life *should* progress. As if there's a predetermined track that everyone runs along at a predetermined pace. Once we unteach ourselves these lies and untruths, we are freed up to live the life that has meaning to us, fulfills us, and brings us joy. Every track of life is unique and makes its own shape. No one runs at the same pace. There are no rules here. We are making it up as we go along. All of us.

Here's who we think you are:
We think you are different from every other soul on this planet. We know you are destined to find joy and love in your life. You are full of fire and capable of doing absolutely glorious things. You are a beautiful, one-of-a-kind, splendid, magical human.

## You Are a Wanderlust Warrior!

I am a Wanderlust Warrior. My path is my own. I may walk with others or I may walk alone, but I go where my questions lead me. I am open to all, beholden to none. I am generous of spirit, fierce of mind. I am strong because my journey is hard. I am slow to anger, but I fight ferociously for what I love. I protect what I value but boldly embrace a worthy risk. I choose truth over comfort. I am a Wanderlust Warrior. My path is my own.

9

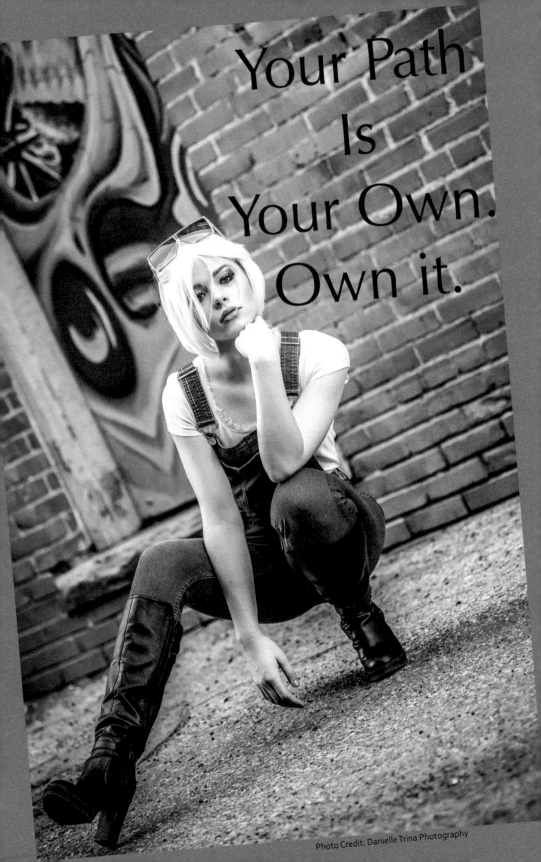

Your Path
Is
Your Own.
Own it.

Photo Credit: Danielle Trina Photography

# HOW TO USE THIS BOOK

There's magic in these pages, and there are a few ways to use this book.

It can be read and the activities completed by you, alone, in your time, and when your mood is up to it. You don't have to share your activities with a single soul. They can be private. Consider this book your Warrior guidebook! And you don't need to read chapters in order. Feel free to jump around and choose the chapter that speaks to you on a certain day. There are no rules here!

This guide can be used in a group of young Warriors. It can be used by schools. Imagine a class dedicated to covering the topics in the book! Or create a Wanderlust Warrior Club. Imagine monthly Tribal Gatherings, where a whole bunch of Wanderlust Warriors come together, working through the chapters as a community. You can invite your friends to discuss the ideas in the book and support each other as you make your way through the chapters and exercises.

Read it yourself, or grab your friends and read together. However you choose to use this book, the most important thing is to have fun with it—challenging fun—and enjoy the process!

You can also do the Walkabout activities that appear in each chapter by yourself or in a group. But first—what exactly *is* a Walkabout?

Walkabout: In Australian Aboriginal society, Walkabout is a rite of passage during which adolescent males, typically ages ten to sixteen, undertake a journey, living in the wilderness for a period as long as six months to make the spiritual and traditional transition into manhood.

No, we are not going to make you live in the wilderness, at least not literally. What the Walkabouts will encourage you to do is to get out of your comfort zone and expand your understanding of the world. So, in a sense, they are little like going into the wilderness—the wilderness of your own soul.

The Walkabout activities range from fairly simple to a little more advanced. You can choose your own adventure, completing one of them or all of them. Again, no rules! The more you do the Walkabouts, the closer you get to the goal of the chapter. Do your thing, Warrior, and make this journey your own!

Photo Credit: Noah P. Gilman Photography

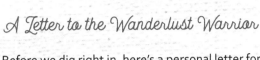

## A Letter to the Wanderlust Warrior

Before we dig right in, here's a personal letter for you, dear girl, from some of your Warrior tribe's members who have gone before you.

Dear Young Warrior,

We are here, right behind you. We are here, on the sides of you. We are here and we will never leave you. We are here.

We watch you as you find your way. With the occasional, pointed finger and outstretched arm we may guide you. But it is up to you, whether you choose that direction.

We teach you what we have learned, but our learnings belong to us, not to you. Life will ultimately teach you in your own time, in your own, unique way.

We want to see you succeed, but our definition of success is the story in our hearts, not yours. How you define your own success is something you alone uncover.

We look on as you rush into your future. We look as you stumble and fall. We will always reach to help you stand, but our arms are not meant to pull you along. We will look to your legs and gently whisper, "Stand, be strong, rise." But our legs are not your legs. You must stand alone.

We see you as you navigate this new world. We see all your experiences and notice all your emotions. We will want desperately to comfort you when the road is hard, and we will. But that is not enough. It will never be enough. You must experience your own discomfort, for it is the price of admission to your meaningful life.

We know you, because we were once you. We know.

You must find your path on your own terms, with your own heart leading you. We will want so much for you, but we know there is very little that we can control. There is only one thing that we promise you: we will be here. We are right behind you. We are on the sides of you. We always will be. But we are not in front of you. We do not block you. Now, run!

Love,
Your Women, Your Tribe

Be strong. For you. For your sisters. For the world.

Photo credit: Danielle Trina Photography

## Chapter 1

*"The Warrior carries her own pack, with strength enough to lend a hand."*

# STAY STRONG

## *Words about Strength from Those Who Have Gone Before You*

There are as many kinds of strength as there are facets to yourself.

Think of any trait you have, any skill, or any fine quality. Each of these, and infinite others you haven't fully realized, can be a source of strength. We are used to thinking about strength of mind, strength of body, strength of spirit. These are important. But where does one kind of strength leave off and the next kind begin? Where does your mind meet your body? And what exactly is spirit, anyway?

These are deep questions. And they probably don't have answers. Because what these questions really do is reveal that our words are blunt instruments, not up to the task of really describing all that is wondrously churning and swirling beneath your surface. You may begin to suspect that things like mind and body and spirit are somehow intertwined, all part of something more mysterious and powerful. So, how do you strengthen important parts of you that you can't even completely describe?

By focusing on *things outside of yourself.* If you are strong, you can make things happen out in the world. If you are strong, you can endure what the world presents to you.

What do you want to make happen? Can you achieve your vision? Then you are strong enough to do so.

What will the world throw at you? Can you handle any challenge? Then you are strong enough to weather it.

And if you *are* strong enough, it's time to raise your gaze, peer farther down your path, and contemplate higher hilltops. If you *are* strong enough, it's also time to look around you, to see who may need help. The Warrior carries her own pack, with strength enough to lend a hand.

Strength is hollow without the will to help others. And the will to help is hollow without strength.

What if you *aren't* strong enough?

Think about things you may not be strong enough to do or to endure. How does that feel? Maybe feeling weak, or vulnerable, is scary. Or depressing. Maybe it feels like a challenge. Whatever it feels like, that's okay. Just make a note of it. It's just information, like finding where you are on a map.

Everybody, in every moment, lives with a different combination of strengths. Some strengths are innate—you are born with them. Some strengths seem to develop without your even thinking about them. Some strengths fade with time or disuse. The point is, strength is different for everyone. Even for just one person, it's different each day.

Complicated, right? That's okay. Keep it simple, again, by focusing on *things outside of yourself*. What do you want to make happen? What will the world throw at you? Test yourself against these things.

In a given moment, faced with a particular task, the strength that serves you may have been inborn, developed naturally, or painfully earned over many years. Any combination will do. Neither the hill you climb, nor the companion you help, will know the difference.

*The Naked Truth*
with Tamara Mellon,
Co-founder of Jimmy Choo,
Accessories Editor for *Vogue*,
Founder of Tamara Mellon shoes

Photo courtesy of Tamara Mellon

Us: Hi Tamara. Thank you for giving us this interview!

T: It's my pleasure. I feel passionately for what you are doing with Wanderlust Warrior Project.

Us: So do we! Should we get right to it?

T: Let's do it!

Us: Please tell us a little about yourself.

T: I'm the founder of Jimmy Choo, and the founder of my new line, Tamara Mellon. As a young girl, I just loved fashion! But I really didn't know what to do with that love. I didn't know what area to go into, and I didn't have a degree from college. So I started in a retail shop, selling clothes. I then went to work for a PR company that made me realize I really wanted to work for a magazine. I went to work at *Mirabella*, where I was the assistant to the fashion director. I built a reputation there. I then headed over to *Vogue* as the accessories editor. I learned a lot at *Vogue*, and one thing in particular really stood out: I learned that shoes were drastically under-branded. Nobody was paying much attention to the shoe. It was kind of like an afterthought. That's when I met Jimmy Choo. At the time he was a just a guy making shoes for private clients in London. He would make them special for photo shoots. We teamed up and the rest is history. The lesson for me was that it doesn't matter if you are not doing the exact thing you want to do, just keep working! You never know what you will learn from it. I learned so many lessons along the way.

Us: Of the book's themes, you embody "strength." Can you tell us what life experiences occurred to get you to embrace your inner strength?

T: Having a really difficult childhood. I grew up with a narcissist mother. It wasn't easy to live with her. I developed some drug issues in my late teens to early 20s. This was back in 1995, in England, and nobody had even heard of rehab. But I went in. I checked in myself. I was determined to change my life. I had no support during this time from my family. I was scared to get old and have nothing if I didn't get help. I was done with living in fear. And fear was my motivator for getting help.

Us: Successful people often get the "What is your greatest advice" question. We're asking it too! What's your best advice for young girls and women?

T: My advice would be that an education is really important. I never went to college, and I did terribly in school. If I had gone to college, I think I would have had more confidence early on. Women have a lot of self-doubt. I think it holds us back. There is this thing called imposter syndrome. I suffered with that, I think a lot of young women suffer with that. Feeling like you don't know what you're doing, so you feel you need to fake it. Men don't have that as much. I think that more women need to speak up in groups and not stay quiet. Learn to speak up and work on self-doubt, that's my advice!

Us: What do you wish you had known earlier in your life that would have made your journey easier?

T: I wish I knew it was okay to ask for help. I always felt like I had to figure it all out alone. Men ask for help all the time. I felt like I was imposing on people if I asked for help. And I also feared that if I asked for help, I would be judged. But the reality is that people really want to help you. I really should have reached out to other men and women earlier in my career.

Us: What do you feel are the biggest obstacles that young women today have to face? How do you perceive most young women reacting to those obstacles?

Photo courtesy of Tamara Mellon

T: I think that women are still facing issues in the work place. We still cannot break through the glass ceiling. Equal pay is a really big issue. Women are getting double the degrees to get the same pay as men. At our first job, we don't have the confidence to ask for what we deserve. We rarely ask for what we need. My advice is to ask for more than you think you deserve. Make sure to get comparisons and know the market. It's so very important to do your research and know what men in your exact job are earning.

Us: What important character traits came most naturally to you, and which took longest to develop?

T: I have always been very persistent. I don't give up. In the beginning I had a lot of fear around what I was doing. I faced the fear and did it anyway. I still really need to work on speaking up! I think it's still an issue for me to speak up, because I still don't value myself enough. I know that sounds crazy given what I have accomplished, but it's true. Another thing that has been hard is trusting my gut. I've had a tendency to think others knew better than I did. I am working on trusting my gut more.

Us: Growing into a young woman, what influences constrained you most, and what influences were most liberating?

T: The external influence that constrained me was my lack of a formal education. What liberated me was having my father in my life. He was very encouraging. It's important to have someone in your corner, and it doesn't have to be your family.

Us: How do you know when you're on track, centered, or moving along your best path? How do you know when you aren't?

T: I really pay attention to the energy of what is going on around me. When I am working with calm focus, I know that it's my best mode. You have to be really careful about who you let into your circle if you are building a team. It's pretty clear when I am not having a good time with the people around me. I really rely on a team of believers. I need positive people. Being around negativity can be crushing. Some people are energy vampires and suck all the good out of you.

Us: What's the hardest decision you made right? What's the easiest decision you made wrong?

T: The hardest decision I ever made was leaving Jimmy Choo. After sixteen years of building a business, I was living in a culture I wasn't happy with. Even though it was my own company! I had to leave because I just didn't recognize my company anymore. The easiest decision that I made wrong was originally taking a lot of money that was offered to me to build the Jimmy Choo brand. I took the money without knowing who I was letting into my inner circle.

19

Us: What do you do/tell yourself when you have moments of self-doubt?

T: I have to be mindful. Once aware that I am experiencing self-doubt, I do breathing exercises and pull myself into a more positive space. Inhale four counts up through my nose, and exhale six counts out through my mouth. Try it! It works!

Us: How much of your success do you sense can be credited to your own values and actions, as opposed to external factors?

T: I think a lot of my success was me. I never gave up, even during the set-backs. I found opportunities when I was young. I was always looking for them. I have a relentless will to win! That stems from my childhood, where I never got the approval I was looking for from my mom. As a result, I felt like I needed to go out into the world to continue to prove myself. I think I am still doing that.

Us: What else should we know about you?

T: Don't let fear cripple you. Everyone is afraid. Be brave and do it anyway! Embrace your fear. Take it with you! Yeah, take fear on your journey. It's coming whether you embrace it or not.

# CHOOSE YOUR STRENGTH ADVENTURE!

## WALKABOUT 1:
### AFFIRMATION CARDS

**Walkabout Directions:**

Have you ever listened to some of the ridiculous stuff your mind tells you? Sometimes it feels like a choose-your-own-adventure in negativity . . . which judgment, label, or self-limiting belief will pop up today?

Well, there's actually some logic to our mind's negative tendencies. The human brain is wired with "negativity bias." Basically, that means in order to survive, we scan for what could go wrong in any given situation. Using this awareness keeps us alive by helping us avoid dangerous situations.

## However!

When negativity becomes a habit, it starts to impact our personal lives in ways that don't serve us. It's our job to notice the habit of our minds and choose another way of thinking. The point of living is not just survival.

Grab some index cards (or make your own) and write your own affirmations on them. You can also use the the affirmation cards we provided for you.

Place the cards in spots in your home that you regularly pass. Each time you see the card, repeat the affirmation out loud to yourself. Notice how it feels when you give yourself encouragement.

They can be anything you want to remind yourself of. What do you need to hear? What do you need to feel? Affirmations are powerful! Search your insecurities and write a message to counter each one of them!

If you want to take this exercise to the next level, repeat the affirmation to your room-mate, sister, mother, or friend. Ask them to hold you accountable to this Walkabout!

# Walkabout 2:
## GET OUT OF YOUR COMFORT ZONE

How do you know when you're playing it too safe?

Life feels a little boring. You are caught in a rut. You are going through the motions. Your schedule might be full, but not fulfilling. You might even be exceptional at what you're doing, yet you feel little satisfaction.

It's important to take on challenges in life that shake things up, get us out of our comfort zone, and make us uncomfortable. Growing pains remind us that we're *growing*.

Getting out of your comfort zone doesn't require you to violate your sense of safety. You don't have to be an adrenaline junkie (though it's cool if that's your thing) to feel alive. Getting out of your comfort zone simply means trying something new, breaking up your routine, and reaching for something that may feel a bit out of your grasp.

In the moment, ask yourself: if you were being heartbreakingly honest, what's something that is holding you back? If you were to let it go, what do you envision would open up in your life?

**In your daily life, get out of your comfort zone by:**

- Raising your hand in class
- Saying hello to someone new
- Asking someone you have feelings for out on a date
- Standing up for yourself
- Owning your feelings and behaviors without blaming anyone else
- Taking a class to build a new skill or to meet new people
- Trying to meditate for fifteen minutes
- Turning off all screens for twenty-four hours

Note: you might need to try something more than once in order to get the full benefit.

## JOURNAL EXERCISE:

You're going to write about your experiences reaching beyond your comfort zone. Write about your setbacks and successes with each attempt. What made the situation especially difficult for you? What personal qualities do you possess that helped you overcome the challenge? What was the biggest lesson you learned about yourself as a result?

```
Write about the first experience out of your
comfort zone.
Date:
What I did and how it felt:
```

Write about the *third* experience out of your comfort zone.
Date:
What I did and how it felt:

Write about the *sixth* experience out of your comfort zone.
Date:
What I did and how it felt:

# WALKABOUT 3:
## DESIGN YOUR OWN SERVICE PROJECT

Once we can take care of ourselves, part of what helps us maintain our strength is serving others. We get stronger when we are of service.

**Choose one of the following activities (or do them all!) to bring a service mentality into your world. You won't believe how good it feels!**

Commit a random act of kindness. Do something nice for someone without expecting anything in return. Some examples: write a sweet message on an index card and leave it in a book at the book store; if you're at the coffee shop, pay for the coffee for the person after you; sweep up the leaves in your neighbor's driveway without telling them; write a secret admirer card for someone and leave it where they will find it. You get the picture, right?

Create a GoFundMe page or a Facebook fundraiser for a cause that touches your heart. The cause can be anything! Maybe you want to raise money for your local animal shelter. Perhaps you are called to raise money for a friend who is ill. You can even raise money to help sponsor someone to go to summer camp. The opportunities here are endless!

Organize a park/beach cleanup with friends. Being of service with your friends can be a ton of fun! You can advertise your cleanup day on social media, post flyers around your town, and even get your local chamber of commerce to help advertise your special service day. And if you are really gutsy and want to go big, let your local TV and newspapers know you are organizing this event. They'll likely cover it and, like presto bananas, hundreds of people might show up and help you clean up the beach or park.

Take on an ongoing volunteer position in your community. But choose one that makes your heart happy. You don't want to volunteer your time for something that you are not passionate about. Some examples: animal shelters, homeless shelters, youth organizations, veterans' centers, elderly care residences.

**CREATE YOUR OWN SERVICE PROJECT!**
**HAVE YOU THOUGHT OF ONE THAT ISN'T ON OUR LIST?**
**GO DO IT! AND GO BIG!**

*JOURNAL EXERCISE:*

What does it feel like to serve? What did you
learn about yourself?

# WALKABOUT 4:
## COMMITMENT

We hear a lot about unconditional love in the self-help world. But what does that even mean, really? To express unconditional love for oneself is to make an absolute commitment to one's own wellbeing. What that really means is that we won't bail on ourselves in difficult moments. We will trust our ability to take care of ourselves, and to maintain progress toward personal goals. But let's be real: it's pretty hard to be there for yourself all the time.

Why is that?

*Think about the different ways you check out on yourself. Usually it's a challenge posed by the people, places, and things in our lives that tempt us to leave the moment, or leave ourselves.*

Get specific—list the stressors in your life.

People:

Places:

Situations:

What does it look like when you bail on yourself?

Sometimes we don't know we've bailed on ourselves until after we've crossed a line, and done something that makes us feel depleted or discouraged. Sometimes we know we're being a bad friend to ourselves, but we do it anyway, out of habit. At other times, we plain don't know any better. But we Warriors learn, tell ourselves the truth and commit to do better next time.

**There are ways to come back to yourself if you've left.**

Daily rituals: Routine and ritual create consistency in our lives. Meditate, burn sage, light a candle with intention, journal, or practice another ritual of your own creation.

Mantra: When we have strayed from self-love, we can use a mantra to help us get back on track. Repeat phrases that help center you, such as "Begin again." "First things first." "Be here now."

Boundaries: If a line has been crossed with a person, place, or thing, what did it teach you? What is the boundary you can create because of that learning experience? It could be something like, "I vow not to gossip anymore because it makes me feel bad."

Self-compassion: Remember that you are only human. Making mistakes is perfectly natural. When we make mistakes, that's the time that we need to love ourselves the very most. Do or say something kind to yourself and keep moving forward.

How do you come back to yourself?

## $\mathcal{W}$ALKABOUT 5:
### INTUITION IS OUR FRIEND

There is a voice inside of us that calls us to our greatest good. Our intuition may start as a whisper and grow louder and louder, until its voice thunders in our ears. Whatever the volume, its presence is a constant. Our internal guide won't stop until we have made the hard choice it's been urging us to make.

Is that voice inside speaking to you now? What risk is it asking you to take? What will you need to let go of? Why is it asking you to let go?

# WALKABOUT 6:
## SLAY SELF-DOUBT

Right before we're about to do something great, or even as we're doing the most mundane things like washing the dishes, we are often visited by self-doubt. It's that voice from within, or the voice resonating from without, that says "You're doing it wrong." Or "Who are you to think you could accomplish such a thing?" As Warriors, we don't let the voice of self-doubt hold us back from our greatness. We've got too much good stuff to do to let that get in the way!

**So, how do we work with this cunning voice? Here's a list of ideas to play around with:**

Awareness. This means paying attention whenever we hear the self-doubt. Examining the source of that particular doubt (parents, ancestors, media, social media, culture, etc.). If it comes from without, firmly look at it and say, "That's not mine."

Nurture yourself like a small child. If the doubt comes from within, talk to your inner child, ask her what she needs, and even take a playful approach to the problem. Solve it like a puzzle.

Disregard negative thoughts. Ask yourself if the thought serves you. If it doesn't, move on and find a thought that does.

Move! Get out of your head and into your body. Take a child's pose. Stand in tree pose for balance. Create your own spontaneous movement.

Pray. This doesn't have to be a prayer to any traditional deity. You don't have to believe in a higher power. Prayer is a set of words that we utter in times when we need hope, support, and strength. Your prayer is a way to connect to the creative spirit inside yourself—the spirit that can manifest anything she dreams.

Create your own secret weapon for dealing with self-doubt. What does that look like for you?

*Your Private Place for*
*Notes or Doodles*

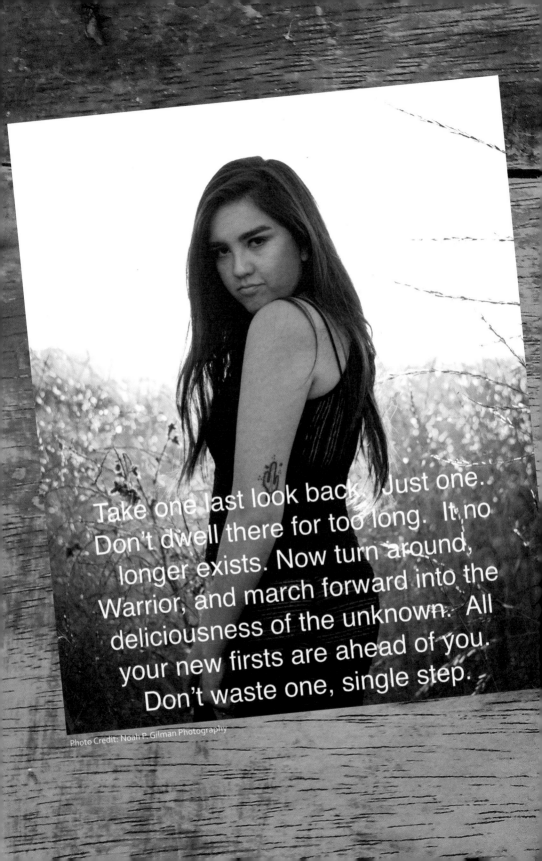

Take one last look back. Just one. Don't dwell there for too long. It no longer exists. Now turn around, Warrior, and march forward into the deliciousness of the unknown. All your new firsts are ahead of you. Don't waste one, single step.

Photo Credit: Noah P. Gilman Photography

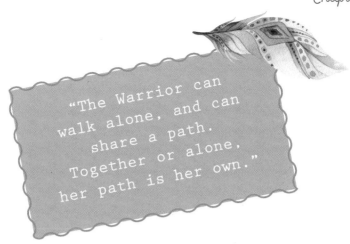

"The Warrior can walk alone, and can share a path. Together or alone, her path is her own."

# BE INDEPENDENT

## *WORDS ABOUT INDEPENDENCE FROM THOSE WHO HAVE GONE BEFORE YOU*

If you are independent, does that mean you are alone? No. It means you *can be alone*, when your path calls for it.

Independence implies the ability to form your own opinions. You may agree with others—that's great! Or you may hold unpopular views. You might even believe things that nobody else seems to think about at all. However your thinking compares with others', independence means that you form your own perspective by making your own judgments. You give your mind and heart the freedom to ask questions, and you come to your own conclusions.

Independence also means having the resources and the will to take action, without requiring the support or permission of others. Others may support you—that's cool! Or they may oppose your plans. Sometimes, others might not even understand your intentions well enough to really oppose them. Whatever reactions others may have, the path your heart and mind direct you to take is your own. You may walk with others or you may walk alone.

How do you know which path is your own? Identifying the right direction requires listening to others, devouring knowledge, trying new things and, above all, paying close attention to how all of your experiences seem to fit in with the story you're writing. The story of your life.

Rarely, but from time to time, your path reveals itself dramatically. The heroes and the villains are easily identified. Your possible paths are clearly laid out. The stakes are high, and you know it.

But it usually doesn't happen like that. Most of the time, everyone around you—and you, yourself—is mixed up in a tangle of heroism and villainy. The paths you might take are twisty and unevenly lit. Judging the consequences of one choice or another requires some guesswork.

When things aren't clear, it's harder to muster the courage to act independently. When the stakes aren't obviously high, it's harder to convince yourself that's it's important to follow your own path. But most of life is filled with undramatic, uncertain moments. And because decision points occur all the time, being tentative can be habit-forming.

The more you choose to pay close attention to people and events around you, the more devotedly you listen to the whispers of your heart and mind, the better equipped you'll be to see the paths before you. Seeing them more clearly, the better able you'll be to act independently. Together, or alone.

Because you are young, it's worth pointing out the difference between independence and contrariness. Contrariness means following a path just because it seems opposite to the popular one. Sometimes, being contrary pays off. In fact, we often celebrate "the rebel" or "the maverick" or "the renegade" precisely because a contrary streak runs through them. But choosing your path by simply opposing the one that everyone else seems to favor is not independence. What path would you choose if nobody else was around? If you need their opinion, if only to oppose it, then you are depending on them. *An independent person may choose to rebel, but not all rebels are independent.*

And sometimes, maybe even frequently, independent people choose to connect with others. They choose community, consensus, agreement and mutual support. The Warrior can draw strength from her tribe. Together with her tribe, she can achieve heights that would be impossible were she alone. The Warrior finds fulfillment in contributing to something larger than herself. Independence is not the same thing as being alone.

But it *can* mean being alone. When your own path requires it.

Photo Credit: Noah P. Gilman Photography

*THE NAKED TRUTH*
with Michelle Rose Gilman,
Founder of Fusion Academy,
Founder of The Well-Heeled
Warrior, Founder of Featherpunk
Studio, Author of The
Wanderlust Warrior Project

Us: Let's get right to it!

M: I'm ready!

Us: Please tell us a little about yourself

M: I am the founder of Fusion Academy, an alternative, one-to-one private middle and high school. Fusion works with students who don't fit within the traditional model of education in our country. Fusion uses the relational approach to teaching. If students feel loved, respected, encouraged and SEEN, they can learn almost anything. I am also a business coach for ambitious entrepreneurs. My coaching business is called The Well-Heeled Warrior. I am an artist (always have been), and I founded Featherpunk Studio, which features hand painted and mosaic musical instruments, jewelry and clothes. I am on the board of directors for many non-profits and one for-profit business. Most importantly, I am mom to Noah, daughter to Linda, and wife to Peter. Oh, and I love a good pair of shoes.

Us: Of the book's themes, you embody independence. Can you tell us more about your independence?

M: My parents gave me a lot of space growing up. Plus, we lived on a tiny, safe island called Key Biscayne. I remember, at a very young age, being out late at night on our bikes, just tootling around. All of the parents on Key Biscayne seemed to allow us all to live a very free life. I am also an only child and spent many hours alone, entertaining myself. I never felt lonely growing up. In fact, quite the opposite. I loved being alone, still do. My parents expected me take care of myself a lot. They owned a bakery and would often be gone from 2am until the afternoon, and then come home and be sleeping by 5pm. If I needed money, I was expected to get a job. If I wanted to buy

Photo Credit: Noah P. Gilman Photography

expensive shampoo, I was expected to pay for it myself. So I learned very early what taking care of my needs meant. Moving into adulthood, I have always done things my way. I might not always have been right, but I lived true. I never had to rely on anyone else financially. This was always very important to me. So I built a life that provided for me. But we have to be careful with being too independent. It can stop you from asking for help when you need it. It can make people believe that you don't need them for much. Which is not true at all. So I have to keep that in check.

Us: Successful people often get the "What is your greatest advice" question. We'll ask it too! What's your greatest advice for young women?

M: Be careful who gives you advice! Really! Consider the source. Have they accomplished a goal that you are working toward? Do they have the life experience to be offering this advice? Are they in a place you one day want to be? Do you admire the life they lead? Here's an example that I stumbled upon while I was wasting too much time on Facebook. I saw an ad for a life coach. She was twenty-three years old and claimed that if you just followed her "proven" steps you could reach all your dreams and become wildly successful. Now, I am sure this young woman believed that her program contained the secrets to life. Yet somehow I just thought, hmmm, I too thought I had it all figured out at twenty-three —but I am now fifty-two and can promise you that my twenty-three year old self had much to learn. Consider the source, ladies! And start learning to trust your gut!

Us: What do you wish you had known earlier in your life that would have made your journey easier?

M: Nothing. Really. I'm not after the easy journey. The easy journey teaches you nothing. If I didn't know something in my early life, I wasn't meant to know it at that

time. I was meant to learn it later. Well, to be completely honest, maybe there is *one* thing that I wish I knew earlier—that I was never as fat as I thought I was, even when I thought I looked like a cow. Which was often. And that took up a lot of my time when I was young.

Us: What do you feel are the biggest obstacles that young women today have to face?

M: There are many obstacles for young women today. Let's start with social media "Influencers." I despise this term. Think about it. What exactly does the word influencer mean? It means just by their sheer presence, strangers are affecting the way you think. About everything. Do young women who pay attention to these folks on social media realize they are being influenced to buy certain things, to accumulate, to dress a certain way? The list is long! And I don't think many young women today realize just how influenced they are by all this. Also, there is simply so much information out there. With all this chatter, are young women coming to their own conclusions about things? Are they curious? Or are they mimicking what they hear, what they see, what they are being told to feel? I think it's a big problem in today's culture. We need to give young women the space to decide for themselves, to encourage them to turn off social media, and turn inward and make their own decisions. That's why this book and movement is so important.

Us: What important character traits came most naturally to you, and which took longest to develop?

M: My ability to form relationships comes really easily to me. I think I am a naturally empathetic person. People open up to me, and for that I am extremely grateful. I also think I have always been naturally creative, and this certainly helps in all areas of life. I see things from various unique angles and want to bring what I see to life! I also pay attention. Specifically, to what might be lacking in the community. Once you figure out what need exists out there, you're one step closer to bringing it to life. One thing that never came naturally to me was obeying rules. I'm not a great rule follower. I find myself asking, "Who made up that life rule?" or "Why are we supposed to do things that way?" As a result, I can be impulsive and act too quickly. I'm still learning how to balance that.

Us: Growing into a young woman, what influences constrained you most, and what influences were most liberating?

M: Can we talk about body issues as a young woman? At an early age, I was very aware of my body. I was overly concerned with how my body looked. Trying to be thin took up way too much energy for me. Trying to look like the models in the magazines, on TV, on the red carpet was very constraining. I went through a period of time when I was purging. I would eat, and then throw it all up. This was in college. That was how desperate I was to remain thin. And now, young women have social media to deal with! I can't even imagine how much worse it would have been for me if I was confronted with Instagram stars, talking to me with their perfect bodies, flawless hair, and runway-perfect outfits!

I'm in my fifties now, and although looking my best is still very important to me, I do it the right way. I exercise at least five days per week, eat healthy, and never step on a scale. It's not about being really skinny; it's now about being really healthy and strong.

When I was a young woman my parents' emphasis on autonomy was extremely liberating for me. I had a lot of support. I was given a lot of freedom and I was able to experience adventures. My folks didn't overprotect me. They let me experience life on my own terms and in my own way. In fact, the minute I left for college, they turned my bedroom into a guest room and put all my stuff in storage. Ha! They might as well have said, "Okay, you're good to go, we believe in you, you believe in you, go live your life!"

Us: How do you know when you're on track, centered, or moving along your best path? How do you know when you aren't?

M: I know I am on-track and centered when things just *flow*. I get in this mode of executing and it seems effortless, not pushed, rushed or hard. There may be hard things I am working on, but the work just flows out of me, and leaves me with a sense of accomplishment and joy. And when I am not centered or moving along my best path, I totally procrastinate. I find myself putting off doing things. I avoid. I zone out and am not focused. *Flow* comes to a jarring halt! When this happens, I force myself to get creative, whether that is painting, gardening, doing mosaics, or simply wrapping a glass jar with burlap and a flower and making a vase. I love the act of creating. And the creations can be teeny things. That helps me.

Us: What's the hardest decision you made right? What's the easiest decision you made wrong?

M: The hardest decision I made right was selling my business when I did. It was a very emotionally difficult thing to do. Fusion Academy was my baby, and it was part of my entire adult life. And I was scared that my identity was so attached to it that I would have a personal crisis when I let go. But that didn't happen. What did happen is that Fusion Academy is now reaching 1000s of kids who need the school, and campuses all over the nation are thriving. At the time of this interview, Fusion is opening its 57th school. It's kind of mind blowing.

The easiest decision I made wrong? I always order the wrong thing at restaurants. It's an easy decision to get wrong! And I get it wrong *all* the time. I know that wasn't the answer you were looking for, but that's all I got for you!

Us: What do you do/tell yourself when you have moments of self-doubt?

M: Everyone has self-doubt. Don't let anyone tell you otherwise. When I doubt myself, I ask, "What's the absolute worst thing that can happen to me?" Then I laugh, because the worst thing has never happened. It's not like an everyday decision I make is likely to end in my death, or the loss of a limb or anything. When the self-doubt kicks in, it stems from a fear of something—usually a fear of what others may think. Once I realize that fear is making me doubt myself, I tell my fear to go sit in a corner. I acknowledge it, then I say it's not driving my bus today!

Us: To which of your own values do you attribute your success?

M: There are a few values that have helped me succeed. I value intimate, raw and deep relationships with others. I truly believe that solid relationships are the cornerstones of real success. There is a saying, "People do business with people they like." That's a good one. But I like to change it to, "People do business with people they love." There isn't a single day that goes by where I don't say "I love you," not only to my family and friends, but to my clients, my co-workers, and executives! It took a while, but now the corporate folks I work with are saying it back to me!

The other value that has really helped me throughout my life is risk-taking. I take a lot of them. I'm not scared of failing. In fact, having a new idea, a new business venture, a new plan is one of the best feelings! Not everything works out the way I want it to, but once a new idea comes to me, I jump straight in.

I have a personal mantra that I say to myself that helps me continue to take risks: "The world can take all the things I have accomplished and created. But no one can ever take from me the things I haven't thought of yet." Doesn't that get you excited? Well, it gets me excited!

Us: How much of your success do you sense derives from your own values and actions as opposed to external factors?

M: I think much of my success comes from my own values, but every successful person has had a "luck moment" drop in their lap. The difference between successful women and unsuccessful women is how they handle the luck drop. Do you snatch up that luck and run with it? Or do you overthink it, wait it out, or do nothing at all with it? In my case, I picked it up and sprinted with it. But if I didn't value confidence, curiosity, independence, and the ability to stray from convention, I wouldn't have been able to do the things I have done.

Us: What else should we know about you?

M: I don't cook. Trust me, you don't want me to. And once I was told I was a bad Reggae dancer. So, there's that.

# CHOOSE YOUR INDEPENDENT ADVENTURE!

## WALKABOUT 1:
### MAKING SPACE

Think of someone you respect who is not like you. They may have different beliefs, values, or approaches to life. Why do you respect them, and why is it important to make space on the path for those who are different than you?

Who is this person?

What makes them different from you?

Why do you respect them?

Why is it important to make space for those who are different than you?

# *W*ALKABOUT 2:
## MINDFUL WALKING — WALKING YOUR OWN PATH

Prepare yourself to take a twenty-minute mindful walk outside. If you are comfortable doing so, please leave your cell phone at home. Before you go, contemplate the following questions:

What do you believe you were born to do on this earth? This doesn't have to be a career aspiration. It can be something like, "I was born to bless this world with my kindness."

What innate gifts do you have that help you walk your path? What makes you unique? What can you say or do to remind yourself of these gifts, and to keep walking when things get difficult?

**Walking Instructions:**

With each step, pause, take a breath, and observe your surroundings. As you move slowly, focusing on the details of your environment, you may notice the chatter of you inner voice. What is it saying? Close your mindful walking experience by looking up at the sky.

What did you experience?

Mindful walking is a practice that helps us stay present on the path. What can this meditative movement help you discover about your life?

# WALKABOUT 3:
## GOING IT ALONE

How often do you do a social activity all by yourself? Probably not very often. Let's get you out doing something alone that you would normally do with others, or currently don't do at all. We know: this one can cause a little anxiety, right? Let's do it anyway!

**Here are some examples:**

- Go to the movies by yourself
- Go have lunch or dinner by yourself
- Go to the beach by yourself
- Go to a park by yourself
- Go to the coffee shop by yourself
- Go to a concert by yourself

```
You get the picture. After you have done this
activity, write down how it made you feel.
The good, the bad and the ugly!
```

# *W*ALKABOUT 4:
## SPEND A DAY BEING A BADASS

Rock stars are rock stars because they are totally committed to their art form. They shred, belt, push the line, and do it all without apology. We idolize them because they spark with our inner badass. We wanna shred too!

We might not have the spotlight or the groupies, but the opportunities to live like a badass are limitless. It's all about confidence, and how we celebrate each moment rather than take it for granted.

**Choose one day this week to live like a badass. Here's what the day can look like:**

When you get dressed, take a look in the mirror before you set out for school or work. Give yourself a "Hell yeah!" You did that! You got dressed like a ninja! Own that! Walk out your door with a little swagger.

Be a smooth driver. Notice what it feels like when you nail the speed limit, make a perfect stop, or slide into that parking spot like it was made for you. Channel your inner Barry White. "Ohhhhhhh yeahhhhhhhh." Don't know who he is? Google that name!

43

# WALKABOUT 5:
## QUESTION YOUR GURUS

Alright, we know you have your favorite role models, maybe even your favorite You-Tube sensations, or Instagram influencers. You probably see and hear from them on a regular basis. There are so many ways they can attract your eyes and ears, right? Sometimes we have a tendency to take everything they say as fact. We might even repeat their views on the world, on fashion, on politics, or even something as simple as which detox is best, or what smoothie recipe rules the world. But we want to challenge you a bit.

**Here's your walkabout, Warrior:**

The next time you listen to a podcast by your favorite motivational person, or listen to your go-to Insta influencer, we really want you to listen to what they are saying. Actively listen. You should take notes about what they are saying. Afterward, ask yourself these questions: Do I believe *everything* they just said? Why? What feels true to me, and how much do I disagree with what was said? If I were to express my thoughts on that topic, what would I say differently? How much do they really know about what they're saying? How would I learn more in order to decide for myself?

Here's space to jot down your observations.

Please do this exercise multiple times. It takes practice to become mindful of the information directed at you.

After you practice over and over again, you will find that you assess the claims people make a little differently. Before, you might have been blindly accepting of everything. And now, you are little more aware of your ability to think for yourself, and you can begin forming your own opinions.

Did that happen to you? Jot down your experience.

YOUR PRIVATE PLACE FOR
NOTES OR DOODLES

The world is BIG. But so am I. And I'm walking straight into it.

Photo Credit: Danielle Trina Photography

"The Warrior believes in her own ability to meet the challenges that her path requires."

# SLAY CONFIDENCE

## *WORDS ABOUT CONFIDENCE FROM THOSE WHO HAVE GONE BEFORE YOU*

Confidence is a precious commodity. Knowing you can trust yourself helps you to unleash your power whenever challenges arise. Confidence feels good. It makes us feel safe, strong and optimistic. And it shows. People are attracted to confidence.

Which is why confidence is so frequently *pretended*.

Spend a day quietly taking notice of how people present themselves. In conversations, advertisements, the choices people make with their clothing, their cars, their posture. Note as well the choices you make. How many of the messages people send—either explicitly or implicitly—are devoted to creating the impression of confidence? How many are calculated to appeal to others' desire for confidence?

You may notice that some people are experts at this game. They craft self-assured personas and wear them very convincingly. You may notice that others seem less expert, revealing their doubts, hesitation and fears for all to see, even as they try not to be transparent. You may notice that you identify more with some people than others.

But how different, really, are the people who present a confident façade from those who reveal their doubt and hesitation? Both feel far less *actual* confidence than they would like to feel. In one way or another, we all feel that way. Or have felt that way.

Or will feel that way. One lesson to be learned from this exercise is that both the pretenders and the obviously fearful deserve your empathy, because each is just another version of yourself.

Another lesson is that *authentic* confidence is far less common in the world than is pretended confidence. True confidence is uncommon. Usually, it is quiet. Confidence doesn't need to announce itself.

Why is real confidence so rare?

Because confidence is what happens when strength meets experience. You are confident when you are strong enough to travel your path, and you have enough experience to know you can handle what the path may bring. This sort of hard-won wisdom takes time. Mistakes must be made, lessons learned, scars earned. Building confidence is hard. And with so many shortcuts tempting you with false promises of an easier way, it's easy to waste time avoiding the work.

What to do in the meantime, as you put in the confidence-building work?

First, understand that a lack of confidence in a particular area isn't necessarily a bad thing. Self-doubt can be a valuable signal that you need to gain strength and experience before you take on a big challenge. It's an invitation to train. It's a signal to prepare—not to give up.

Second, pay attention to your natural responses to risk. Different people have different impulses in the face of risk. Some people instinctively avoid it, seeking safety instead. Risk-avoidance is not a sign that you lack confidence, though it may feel like it. Others instinctively embrace risk, spurred on by a rush of excitement. Risk-seeking is not confidence, though it may feel like it.

Most of us fall somewhere in between these two extremes. Neither response is superior—each has its advantages, depending on the situation. Most important is to become expert at detecting your own impulses, so you can take them into account before making key decisions.

Finally, use your tribe. Your tribe has strengths and experiences that you, as an individual, do not (yet) have. By looking to others who are worthy of your trust for help and guidance, you extend your power to wider spheres. At the right times, and for the right reasons, your tribe can supply any confidence you lack.

## The Naked Truth
with Katherine Ross,
Senior Executive at
Louis Vuitton and Hermès,
Senior Vice President of
Communications at Prada,
Co-Founder **re:la** (regarding
Los Angeles) clothing brand

Us: Thank you for being part of the Wanderlust Warrior Project!

K: It's a wonderful concept.

Us: Thank you! Ready for your interview?

K: Yup!

Us: Please tell us a little about yourself.

K: I am a communications consultant in the fashion and luxury market. I curate the on-going Wear LACMA fundraising project that works with Los Angeles-based designers to benefit the Los Angeles County Museum of Art. Most recently, I have launched a new clothing project with a partner called **re:la** (regarding Los Angeles), which celebrates the culture of Los Angeles. I have consulted for Nicolas Ghesquière while he was at Balenciaga as well as other luxury brands such as Hermès and Louis Vuitton. I am a former senior executive at LVMH Moët Hennessy Louis Vuitton, a leader in the luxury business that possesses a unique portfolio of over 60 prestigious brands. I worked with many of the designers for those brands on strategic communications and reported directly to the chairman, Bernard Arnault. Prior to my work at LVMH, I was Senior Vice President of Communications for Prada. At Prada, I worked directly with Miuccia Prada and opened the Rem Koolhaas- designed epicenter stores for the brand. Preceding my work in fashion, I was an executive at Sotheby's in New York, working in business development where I started the Museum Services Department.

I lived in New York until 2006, when we moved to Los Angeles for my husband's new position as the CEO and Director of the Los Angeles County Museum of Art.

Us: Of the book's themes, you embody "confidence." Please tell us what life experiences you've had that helped you embrace your inner confidence.

K: Well, I hope I am all of the themes that your book describes. In order to achieve goals, one needs to be strong, independent, confident, kind, brave and curious. I know that I possess social intelligence and I always try to patient and kind with others. You never know when and where you will see them again.

I was a Drama major at UCSD [University of California, San Diego], and when I got out of school I immediately went to work, the day after graduation, in Los Angeles at The Greek Theatre. I continued to study acting in the evenings. I went on auditions and I found that all the work I had put into learning the craft of acting was really not resulting in actual *work as an actress,* which was very disappointing. I went to London to visit a friend and walked into Sotheby's. It was very exciting to watch an auction in the salesroom. I thought, I can really do anything I want, and maybe there are other things out there that are exciting, where my talents as a person will be rewarded. I came back to Los Angeles, packed my bags and moved to New York. Originally it was my plan to go to graduate school at NYU in arts administration. However, within a month I was working at Sotheby's, managing the tickets for the auction house sales of Impressionist, Contemporary and Latin American art. I think it was all the themes that you describe that gave me the courage and confidence to take that risk and make a change.

I worked at Sotheby's for sixteen years. Although I learned so much at Sotheby's and loved my colleagues and the challenges of the work, at about the twelfth year I was really feeling undervalued, and thought it was time for a change. However, I was able to wait and really excel at Sotheby's for a few more years. Waiting an extra four years provided me with an opportunity to really be in the right place and right time and have had the right kind of exposure to a bigger cultural world, and the confidence to make a big change into the world of fashion.

Photo Courtesy of Katherine Ross

Us: Successful people often get the "What is your greatest advice" question. We'll ask it too! What is your greatest advice for young women?

K: Life has its ups and downs, and it is really how you ride the wave that counts. I always try to keep my own counsel and be calm in a storm. I think sometimes it is very difficult to do that—you want to tell your friends or colleagues, to relieve yourself from the stress of keeping it all inside. If you do decide you need to talk to someone, just pick one person that you really trust. I usually find that if you ride the wave and remember that you are a strong, confident, brave person, that you will enjoy the ride—even when it is heading south! Remember: the only way from down is up, and the only way from way up on that pedestal is down.

Us: What do you wish you had known earlier in your life that would have made your journey easier?

K: I don't really have regrets . . . and my journey was filled with ups and downs. I learned a great deal going through them. I think if I knew that I would not get married until I was forty-three . . . then I would not have wasted all that time dating!

Us: What do you feel are the biggest obstacles that young women today have to face? How do you perceive most young women reacting to those obstacles?

K: I think women should not take anything for granted—discrimination is alive and well in our world and we need to be a voice for change. I am not politically minded, but I want my girls (I have a teenage daughter and a step-daughter that is in her early twenties) to speak their mind and stand up for themselves in their lives.

Us: What important character traits came most naturally to you, and which took longest to develop?

K: I like people, so I have pretty good social abilities and I am a natural communicator. My confidence level goes up and down, but on average it is above normal, which certainly helps when communicating with strangers.

I think I was not always so curious as a young person, but it seems to grow as I get older. Now that I am over fifty, I am curious about almost everything.

Us: Growing into a young woman, what influences constrained you most, and what influences were most liberating?

K: I grew up in Michigan and I found that staying in Michigan was constraining me. I left Michigan after my sophomore year in college to go to University of California. I really felt, as a young person, this need to create my own path. Moving to California certainly liberated me both physically and emotionally, and then moving to New York City at twenty-four years of age liberated me even more. I think the environment you live in and the people you surround yourself with have a tremendous impact on you.

Us: How do you know when you're on track, centered, or moving along your best path? How do you know when you aren't?

K: I think if one is calm in a storm then you are always on track and centered. When things constantly seem to be pushing you off course, it is time to re-evaluate. I think as you get older and more experienced with this, it becomes easier to navigate.

Us: What do you do or tell yourself when you have moments of self-doubt?

K: Stay strong and carry on! I say "I love you" to myself.

Us: To which of your own values do you attribute your success?

K: I know how important it is to be strong, confident, kind and creative. I think that the fact that I do not always fit in with everyone makes me feel special, and that has helped me along the way.

Us: How much of your success do you sense derives from your own values and actions as opposed to external factors?

K: I think it is fifty-fifty. Much of my success is from my own hard work and staying the course when things seemed not always so great. At the same time, I feel that the external factors and things that lead someone to one place or another can hold equal weight.

Us: Thank you! You rock!

# CHOOSE YOUR CONFIDENT ADVENTURE!

## *W*ALKABOUT 1:
### WARRIOR PAINT

Our face is the first thing that people see when they look at us. It's our first shot at letting people know who we are. We can spend a lot of time covering up our imperfections with makeup, and sometimes we do. But our face is one of our main storehouses of expression. It's how we story tell, communicate emotion, display our connection. What if, instead of make-up, you painted your face with your Warrior beauty? What if you took your life experiences, the things inside of you that want to be set free—the stuff that makes you, you—and positioned them on the canvas that is your precious face?

You can do this several different ways using the image of a face below (or use a photograph of your own face).

**Here's way number one:**

Use this list of words and write one, some, or all of them where you feel they best fit on the face.
- Funny
- Sweet
- Helpful
- Thoughtful
- Intuitive
- Expressive
- Friendly
- Fierce
- Sensitive
- Careful
- Skeptical
- Wild
- Shy
- Rebellious
- Your own words here _____ 55

**Here's way number two:**

Gather some magazines or other printed media and tear out images or words or colors that represent who you are. Glue or staple them on to the face.

**Here's way number three:**

Use markers, crayons, gel pens, pencils and whatever else you desire and go to town on the face. Make it a mask that represents who you are and who you want to present to the world.

**Here's way number four:**

Have a better idea for your face? Go for it and have fun!

We know that you're not going to walk out of the house with words and images pasted all over your real face (nor would we ever ask you to!), so when you do go out into the world, what will you do to signal to those around you who you really are, and what you're really about?

Journal your thoughts here:

# *W*ALKABOUT 2:
## POSITIVE SELF-TALK

In moments when we're upset, uncertain, or feel self-doubt, we can still choose to be there for ourselves. Here is a practice that you can use when those feelings rise up in you. Close your eyes and place your hand over your heart. What do you notice with this gesture? Anything? Nothing? Again, no judgement from us!

What do you feel?

Add a mantra to the gesture by saying, "(Your name), I am here for you." Hang out in that feeling for a few moments. Come back to this practice whenever you need to feel reassured. Did that change your experience? Do you feel different? Better? Worse?

Journal it!

# WALKABOUT 3:
## SELF-REFLECTION

It's often said, "The eyes are the window to the soul." Have you ever spent time staring into your own eyes? A lot can be revealed when we look deeply into ourselves. And to tell you the truth, this exercise can be rather trippy!

Look into a mirror close enough so you can see only your eyes. Set a timer for five minutes and stare into your eyes until you hear the alarm ring (it will feel like forever!).

What were the obvious or unexpected things you noticed simply by looking into your own eyes?

# WALKABOUT 4:
## TIME TRAVEL

If you were to travel fifty years into the future and visit your future self, what would she thank you for doing in your current life? What are you doing today (think habits, choices, commitments, adventures) that is contributing to a better life in your future?

What are some things you are doing today that your future self might say didn't help her achieve her dreams?

Is there anything you can change now, so that your future self can thank you?

YOUR PRIVATE PLACE FOR
NOTES OR DOODLES

Maddie Finch
9/23/98 - 1/1/18

Photo Courtesy of the Finch family

"With empathy and an open heart, The Warrior embraces a fellow traveler in need of compassion and love."

# KINDLY BE KIND

## *Words about Kindness from Those Who Have Gone Before You*

Yellowed by a thick coating of dust, a lizard skitters across the baked earth in front you. Fluidly writhing across the flats, it taunts you with its inexplicable energy. You raise your eyes to the horizon, squinting against the intensity of a merciless sun. Heat rises in waves from the cracked and sterile terrain, blurring air as dry as the bones of the fallen. The remains of travelers who came before you litter the path, mocking your journey with skeletal grins. Through the shimmering haze, you make out . . . nothing. The path extends to the limits of your vision, disappearing into a featureless line where desert meets sky.

Your water flask gave up its last drops hours ago. Your boots have worn nearly through and admit the painful insults of each hot shard of stone underneath your every step. Step after endless step.

Despite its mocking, you are grateful to have glimpsed the lizard. Despite the cruelty of their silent laughter, you are grateful for the bones of the fallen. For these are your only companions, the only distractions from the murmurings of your mind. Murmurings that no longer take the form of words, but a dull hum that seems to rise and fall with the dark tide of your fear.

*Why have I chosen this hopeless path?*

This question takes hold in your mind. Treading blindly now, with closed eyes, each step seems more pointless than the last. Somewhere within your core, from a place deeper than you knew you had, you consider giving up. So easy, to collapse where you stand. To rest and take your place among the fallen.

You stumble. Opening your eyes once more to the angry sun, you see that the ground, flat and barren for numberless miles, has unexpectedly broken into a steep decline. So abrupt was the change it was invisible from a distance. You struggle to negotiate the slope, focused entirely on your footsteps.

*What's that sound?*

With an effort, you halt your descent. Hands on knees, you sway for a moment, catching your breath. Finally, you raise your head.

A hidden valley. Deep and narrow, its walls largely block the sun, creating long swathes of shade. At the bottom, a stream. Shallow, but swiftly flowing, its waters run clear and burble audibly.

*That was the sound.*

Slowly, you advance toward the stream, hesitant to accept what your eyes and ears take in. Reaching the valley floor, you hug the wall, accepting its gift of shade. The valley narrows towards a bend in the stream. On the far side of the water, a lizard basks in the sun, shimmering as droplets of water reflect the light. Washed clean of its dusty coating, the lizard's skin radiates a lush, emerald green.

Arriving at the bend, you turn the corner. A lone palm spreads its fronds, sheltering both sides of the stream with its shadow. Entirely still just a moment before, the fronds bend now, bowing to acknowledge a passing breeze. Bowing with them, you kneel to the stream's edge. You dip cupped hands into the flow, then raise them to pour cool water over your head, rivulets streaming down your neck and back.

Turning to the palm, you face the valley wall before you. There, scratched onto its stony surface, is a map. And below the map, a message. From one of your tribe. One of your sisters, who traveled this path before you. One who, perhaps long ago, suffered and endured as you have. And conquered her own dark tide.

Kindness is a stream in a hidden valley. A patch of unexpected shade. A merciful breeze.

Kindness is a gift to a lonely, fearful traveler. It creates hope. It reveals possibility.

Kindness is a sister, a friend, a voice of welcome and encouragement—when none seems possible.

Kindness, Warrior, is grace in the presence of vulnerability. And it is one of your most powerful skills. How many times in your life would a simple kindness have lifted you, immeasurably, had it only been offered? What would that kindness have been worth?

We are all, *every one of us*, travelers on an arduous path. We are all vulnerable, each in our own ways, at our own times, on our own path. Pay attention, and infinite opportunities for kindness will reveal themselves to you. Endless occasions on which you can transform, often easily, the experience of a sister, and give her shade, shelter, hope.

Because most suffering is silent, endured alone—even when the afflicted person is surrounded by others—it is easy to pass over these opportunities. And because kindness confronts us with the truth that we, too, are vulnerable, it is easy to withhold. We prefer to feel strong rather than face our own dark tide.

Most kindness goes ungiven. On your own path, how many opportunities for kindness have escaped your notice, simply because you paid no attention? How many opportunities have you clearly seen, but allowed to pass? What prevented you from acting? What kept you from helping your sister?

Kindness is easy to withhold but doing so comes at a price. And not just for the lonely, fearful traveler in need. The price is paid by your sense of self-worth. Always.

A kindness given benefits not only your sister, but also yourself. By offering grace to the vulnerable, you make yourself worthy to receive grace in your own defenseless moments. Worthy, not because it's practical, and one good turn deserves another, although that is also true. Kindness makes you worthy of kindness because, in a deep sense, you are your sister. Her suffering is your suffering. Her hope is your hope.

As Warriors, we fight the dark tide together.

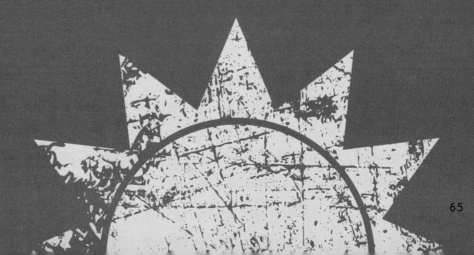

A note about this interview. Maddie Finch, nineteen, was brutally murdered at her home on January 1st, 2018, at her own New Year's Eve Party. The family found a short poem that I wrote. Here is the poem.

## THE NAKED TRUTH
with Carrie Walkington Finch,
Mom, Teacher

She had a gypsy soul
and a Warrior Spirit.
She made no apologies
for her wild heart.
She left normal
and regular to
explore the
outskirts of
magical and
extraordinary.

And she was
glorious.

- Michelle Rose Gilman

Photo Credit: Noah P. Gilman Photography

The poem is engraved on her headstone, a memorial plaque, and on T-shirts the family wore. They felt that the poem described their Maddie. I found this family by chance. I never knew Maddie when she was alive. But I have gotten to know her family. This interview is different. This interview is with her mother, speaking on behalf of her daughter. What I have found was that Maddie was on her way to becoming a lighthouse of a Wanderlust Warrior. One part kind, one part a bit rebellious, one part loving, one part lost, one part courageous, and many parts curious. I can honestly say that I now know Maddie. I have her mom to thank for this. Here is our interview.

Us: Thank you Carrie, for this interview!

C: I'm honored to be here and be involved with this!

Us: Thank you!

Us: Let's talk about Maddie. We know this is hard for you.

C: It's hard, but I'm glad you are keeping her life alive by including her in your book.

Us: This isn't the normal interview. We know her life was cut short by a horrible incident. We want to honor her, and you, her mother.

C: Thank you. Really.

Us: Okay, let's get started.

C: Ok.

Us: Can you tell us about Maddie?

C: Maddie was our second child. Due to some medical issues, we weren't supposed to have Maddie. It was too risky, but we went ahead with it. She was born three weeks early, and she was so chubby! She was the best baby ever. She smiled early, played by herself and was easy from day one. Things changed when she was a toddler. She was a spitfire and remained that way until she left us. She took up lots of space and was always needing things.

As Maddie grew up, she found it really hard to compete with her older sister, Josie. Josie always got straight A's, and she was a starting athlete. So Maddie decided to take a different approach and make a commitment to be in the band. Of all the instruments she could have chosen, Maddie decided on the tuba! The tuba! The thing was simply way too big for her. No other girls played the tuba. But that is exactly why Maddie chose it! She wanted to stand out. She always wanted to do things other girls weren't doing. Maddie also picked up sports and was the catcher in softball. She also got into karate. I remember her being so proud when she knocked out a fifth grade boy! They named her Ninja! Once again, here she is standing out and not doing things the other girls were doing.

When Maddie got to high school, she had a rough go of it. She struggled with many medical issues. She had kidney stones and was often in the hospital. She struggled with being sick all the time. She was always in pain. Looking back, it was probably fibromyalgia.

Emotionally, Maddie also struggled. She had a hard time finding her way. She didn't really care about school, although she was always very intelligent. She really focused in on people. She desperately wanted people to need her, so she befriended many kids who were having a hard time. She wanted to save them. She was drawn to friends who were older than she was. She seemed to be more adult than her peers. What Maddie really wanted to do was start living her life. One of her friends died of stomach cancer, and ever since then, Maddie always said she wanted to be a pediatric nurse in oncology. Her dream was to travel to Africa, be a nurse there and adopt kids.

Us: Tell us more about her friends.

C: Maddie had friends all over the place. From all walks of life. She put many miles on her car traveling to friends from various different regions. She helped these friends when they were in dark places, then she would move on to the next person who needed her. She was always helping someone in need. I never knew just how many people she touched until her memorial visitation. We live in a very small town of 1200 people. 1500 people came to her visitation. I had no idea how she knew all of these people. Some of those kids came to me during the visitation and said, "Maddie appeared in my life when I needed someone the most," and "Maddie was there when I was in my darkest days." I also heard, "Maddie was the most generous person I have ever known." I don't think I ever would have known this about her if she hadn't died.

Us: How was Maddie at home?

C: Very different than how those friends saw her! Maddie had a fierce, rebellious side to her. She could get angry and sometimes very mean. I think that she gave so much of herself to other people that when she came home, she didn't have anything left. She was tough. There were plenty of arguments. I think she felt trapped in our small town and desperately wanted to be independent and on her own. But once college started, all of that changed. We saw a sweet side to her. She got along great with her sister. She had grown up.

Us: What did she excel at?

C: Oh my! Maddie was so incredibly creative! She was a wonderful artist and writer. And she could put an outfit together like nobody's business! She loved fashion. She loved photography. She was always taking pictures of her friends. She also loved to rescue dogs. She rescued a pitbull. She volunteered at the hospital in the Alzheimer's unit. She was great at it, but it often broke her heart. She would go and work with those patients, do amazing things with them, and then show up the next day and they didn't have any idea who she was. She eventually stopped volunteering there. I think she was looking for relationships, but she couldn't have any with that population.

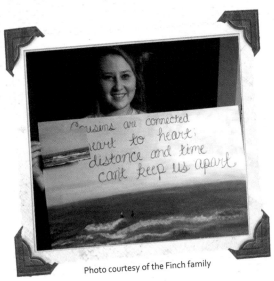

Photo courtesy of the Finch family

Us: Are you comfortable telling us about the day she died?

C: Yes. Maddie asked if she could have a New Year's Eve party at our house. We were all concerned because, a year prior, she had thrown a party and the house got trashed. It was a disaster. Of course, we grounded her then, we even went to therapy for a while. So you can imagine that we weren't thrilled when she wanted to have another party. But we really saw a new Maddie that past year and we agreed,

Beauty is in the voice of a girl
who speaks the truth
even though she shakes.
Beauty is in the eyes of a girl
who sees things
most people try to hide
Beauty is in the hands of a girl
who uses them
to help others up
Beauty is in the mind of a girl
who knows who she is
And knows it's enough.

Photo courtesy of the Finch family

with some really strict rules. Maddie took lots of precautions for the party. She shuttled people in. She would be taking their keys so they didn't drive drunk. Many friends were going to spend the night.

My husband and I were going to go out to dinner and stay at a hotel that night. The last time we ever saw Maddie, she looked so beautiful and happy. So we left. That night her dad called her and all seemed to be fine. We went to sleep at about 10:00 p.m. Then, the strangest thing happened. My husband must have been having a nightmare because he basically punched me in his sleep! We both woke up, and my husband said that he was dreaming that someone was hurting Maddie and asked if we should go home. We didn't, but I wish we would have.

At about 1:00 a.m, the phone started to ring. It was our next-door neighbor. He said, "Jason, this is Kevin, and I need you to come home. It's Maddie, Jason." Then my phone started ringing and it was Maddie's best friend. "Carrie, it's really bad and you need to come home right now. There's lots of blood." But nobody was telling us what was going on! All we knew was that something terrible had happened. We got ourselves into the car. I don't remember much of the drive at all. But I do remember the phone was constantly ringing. The EMT from town called. And I was screaming questions into the phone. "Where are you taking her? What happened? We'll meet you at the hospital, just tell us where you're taking her!" All he said was that we should pull over and that they would come and pick us up. Pick us up? I didn't understand. And then it hit me. "Jason, they're not taking her anywhere!" My husband screamed so loud.

We reached the house, but it was difficult to get there because of the cops and EMTs everywhere. Maddie's car was parked in the driveway. The EMT told us not to go inside, but Jason did. And there he saw her face. She was lying on the floor in the garage. And the blood. She had been shot. But nobody was telling us anything about what happened.

69

We eventually found out it was a young man in a gang who had shot her. To this day, we still don't have the details. But the case is still ongoing. We pray for justice every day. But nothing will bring our Maddie back to us. It's been eight months since she was murdered. Most days I don't function at all. No, not at all.

Us: Thank you, Carrie. Thank you for feeling comfortable sharing your tragic and heartbreaking loss.

Us: What do you think she would want all young women to know?

C: Two things, I think. First, it's better to be the one who smiles than the one who didn't smile back. She would want them to know that they need to love themselves. She would say that it is a hard thing to do. She really worked on it, but she compared herself to her sister and other girls. It was hard for her to love her body.

Us: What do you think, if Maddie had known it earlier in her life, would have made her journey easier?

C: I think if she would have had the self-confidence to love herself more. She knew that was her weakness. She was on the path [toward greater] self-confidence by playing the tuba, by conquering her goals. She was trying to better herself. She was just starting to see how she fit in life before her life was taken. Maddie loved so hard and so much and she wanted that in return.

Us: What do you think Maddie would feel are the biggest obstacles that young women face?

C: Small towns are limiting for young women. She felt limited. She would often find ways to stir life up so she could experience a wide range of emotions.

Us: How would you like Maddie to be remembered?

C: I hope the world remembers Maddie's very large heart. She had a soft spot for the underdog. I hope they remember her kindness, her accepting nature, her quick wit, deep soul and her unwavering love for people. She had a vision about how the world needed to be. She was working on how to put a piece of herself on it.

Us: Thank you, Carrie. Your family will forever remain in our hearts.

don't forget how to love. Love is one of the most complex, yet simple things in the universe. True love is hard to come by. Don't throw it out, work for it. In the end, love is the thing that will lift your spirit + carry your soul when you feel like your world is crashing down like tidal waves. Let love lift you. Let love make you fly, especially when everything else is weighing you down.

Photo courtesy of the Finch family

# CHOOSE YOUR KINDNESS ADVENTURE

## WALKABOUT 1:
### SYMPATHETIC JOY

Sympathetic joy happens when we allow ourselves to experience happiness for someone else's success, even if they have something we feel we lack in our own lives, like a romantic relationship, a cool job, or a fun family life. When we celebrate others' happiness, we shift from a scarcity perspective (i.e., we feel we don't have enough) to an abundance perspective—we know there is enough joy for everyone.

Can you text two people in your life right now, and tell them you are happy for something positive they have in their life? Pause after you send each text. How do you feel when you express sympathetic joy?

## WALKABOUT 2:
### KINDNESS RECEIVED

Recall a time someone surprised you with their kindness. Was the kindness directed toward you, or toward someone else? What about this experience stands out to you as special? How can it inspire your own willingness to be kind?

For the next week, we want you to email three people, first thing in the morning. There doesn't have to be a reason for this email. Just think of the first three people who pop into your head. The email should be a very simple one. It just reads something like this:

*Hey (name),*

*Just popping by to let you know that I was thinking of you today. Hope you are well.*

Or

*Hey there (name),*

*Wanted to send a quick email to let you know that you popped into my head today. I was just thinking about the time that we [insert activity: went to that concert, had dinner at _____, took a walk] and it brought a smile to my face. Have a great day!*

See? Simple?

```
How did sending those emails feel to you?
Did you get a response back? Journal your
experience.
```

# WALKABOUT 3:
## CONSCIOUS CONSUMING

When we talk about consuming, we tend to think about the things we eat. Women spend a lot of time thinking about what they eat and all that goes along with that. But consuming means so much more than how we fuel our bodies. It is the energy that we allow ourselves to take in—the media we watch or listen to, who we follow on social media, where we let our conversation wander. All of the information we absorb impacts our mood and our friendliness. Have you ever noticed what you feel and talk about when you read celebrity gossip or watch reality TV shows that pit women against each other? What does it do to your energy? What do you think prompts you to consume those things?

Track your emotions based on your consumption of certain media. See how your feelings and perceptions change after each item you consume. Adjust your consumption accordingly.

```
Today I watched:
and it made me feel:



Today I listened to:
and it made me feel:



Today I read:
and it made me feel:



Today I watched:
and it made me feel:



Today I listened to:
and it made me feel:
```

Today I read:

and it made me feel:


Today I watched:

and it made me feel:


Today I listened to:

and it made me feel:


Today I read:

and it made me feel:


Today I watched:

and it made me feel:


Today I listened to:

and it made me feel:


Today I read:

and it made me feel:

# WALKABOUT 4:
## COMPASSION PRACTICE

Compassion is more than a feeling of empathy. It is a movement of the heart. Often, the things that break our hearts are the very things that compel us to make a difference in the world. We realize our hearts weren't shattered, only broken open.

Can you think of a heartbreak in your life that has helped you experience more empathy and connection for others? Write it down.

Think of a heartbreak in your community or the world that touches your heart. Because compassion is an act and requires movement, it beckons us off the couch or away from the screen. Every day for two weeks, do an act—big or small—that will serve a single person, small community, or the world at large. Write what you did in the box.

How did your acts make you feel?
Would you consider continuing this practice?

# ACTS of COMPASSION

|  | Week 1 | Week 2 |
|---|---|---|
| MONDAY |  |  |
| TUESDAY |  |  |
| WEDNESDAY |  |  |
| THURSDAY |  |  |
| FRIDAY |  |  |
| SATURDAY |  |  |
| SUNDAY |  |  |

*Your Private Place for Notes or Doodles*

The universe is a toybox.
What toys will you find, and how will you play?

Photo credit: Danielle Trina Photography

"The Warrior sees through sparkling distractions, into deep waters. She hears intelligence whispering beneath forceful voices."

# INTEL ON INTELLIGENCE

## *Words about Intelligence from Those Who Have Gone Before You*

It is possible to spend a lifetime scratching mostly at the surface of things. You'll get by. You might even, in many ways, be "successful." In an advanced society, surrounded and supported by so many layers of protection and guidance, it is possible to leave the noticing, the thinking, and the true understanding to others.

Unless, that is, you are a Warrior.

Warriors may appreciate things that dazzle, allure, enrage or entertain. But only for a moment. Soon, they grow tired or bored with the show. They ask, "But what have I learned?"

A Warrior hungers for what lies beneath. She seeks the ideas that drive all the action. She looks for similarities among the diverse, and for differences within all the sameness. And she is never fooled by a new coat of paint.

A Warrior consumes knowledge. She is a connoisseur of its quality, careful not to put faith in just any claim. She demands evidence to back any belief, from herself as well as others. No idea is above questioning. Not even one.

A Warrior appreciates that knowing is not the same as understanding. "Smart" is not the same as intelligent. Smart can draw a map from memory. Intelligent examines the map, deciding which valleys may be the most fertile.

Intelligence makes the most of ideas and information. You already possess an awe-inspiring tool, the most wondrous and complex organ known to humankind—your brain—which is engineered to do just that. Better than any other kind of creature that has ever lived. Even on the days you feel dullest and clueless, your brain is a magnificent stallion.

Feed the stallion. Groom it. Train it. Then mount your stallion and let it run. It will take you far, and to unimagined, wondrous places. But only if you feed, groom, and train it well.

Here's an important secret to unleashing your inner Warrior intelligence: *Learn what to ignore.*

Nothing stands in the way of intelligence so much as distraction. At the simplest level, everyday distractions like excess noise and light, chatter and clutter, tie up your brain's machinery and cause it to expend energy on fruitless tasks. Your mind has all the power it needs to attack the problems you face—if you let it. Create the space for powerful thinking. Space in your schedule, and space in your physical setting.

Distraction can also come from deep within. Anxiety, exhaustion, excess pride, envy, impatience, fear, anger . . . these are powerful conditions. They grip both body and mind (and what exactly is the difference between these two, anyway?). They fracture your attention. You are human, Warrior, so you'll never be free from these disruptive influences, nor should you be free from them. They serve their purposes. But learn to sense when they are operating within you. Call them out—name them! That act alone limits their ability to distract. Left to their own devices, they spin webs in the dark. They encumber your intelligence.

The world of messages that surrounds you constantly offers distractions. Advertisements appeal to your emotions. People and groups cast you in roles you're not prepared or willing to play. News is delivered to outrage you more than to enlighten you. Technology is engineered to hold you hostage, engaging your attention for its own benefits—not for yours.

Your attention is a precious commodity, Warrior. It is limited, even rare. Many forces will compete for your attention, with cunning, charisma, and unrelenting effort. Will you give your attention away so easily? Or will you invest it wisely? Will you allow your stallion to languish, trapped in its stable? Or will you free your stallion to run? Most important, do you have the self-awareness to know which of these you are doing?

The world rushes in on us. It always will. Unfiltered, the rush of experience distracts you, leaving your intelligence no clear and worthy targets. But over time, experience will teach you what to ignore. You'll be able to channel the rushing flow. Over time, your intelligence will build a detailed model of the world. A model that serves you. And is worthy of your attention.

## *The Naked Truth*
### with Ayse P. Saygin, Ph.D.,
Associate Professor of Cognitive Neuroscience and Neuropsychology at University of California, San Diego

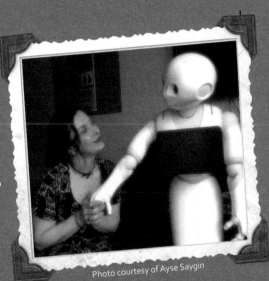

Photo courtesy of Ayse Saygin

Us: Hi Ayse! Thank you for being part of our project.

A: Happy to do it.

Us: Let's get right to it. Can you tell us a little about yourself?

A: I am a professor of cognitive neuroscience and neuropsychology at University of California, San Diego, where I previously completed my Ph.D.. Before that, I studied computer science and mathematics. I was born in Turkey and, except for a year when I was an exchange student in a small town in Texas, went to school there, including college and a Master's degree. I moved to San Diego for my Ph.D., then to London as a post-doctoral researcher, after which I got a job at U.C. San Diego. It is rare to get a faculty position where you get your Ph.D., but it in my case it happened. Since 2009, I have worked at U.C. San Diego, where I teach, run a research lab, and have way too much to do! I'm forever behind.

I wanted to be a scientist from a very young age. At the age of about four, when people asked what I wanted to be when I grew up, I would answer, "a man job," which sounds more grammatical in Turkish. My mother was a clinical psychologist, my father an electrical engineer. So I may have associated science, technology, engineering, that sort of thing, with men. And perhaps I had inferred from society that people in those sorts of professions (predominantly men) had more freedom and independence. Over the years, my inherent interest in stereotypically male things remained, and gained more meaning as I grew up. But from early on, I wasn't a very gendered child.

It was not a direct path to what I am doing today. Originally, I wanted to be a physicist or a biologist. Physics—especially astrophysics, and when I got older, quantum physics—fascinated me. On the other hand, the 1980s and early 90s were a big time for genetics, which also caught my attention. I was a curious child who loved to learn. Fortunately, my family was supportive. I read very broadly, had a computer, and would do experiments at home.

The education system in Turkey was quite different from that in the U.S. Students chose a track pretty early on. Even though I had other interests (literature, music, art), I always chose the science track. In college, I ended up majoring in mathematics, however. I accidentally scored a bit higher than I expected in the university entrance exam, a highly competitive, three-and-a-half-hour test that was offered only once a year and determined your university and your major. When I found out the exam results, I was in tears. Mathematics would be a great basis for the rest of my education and career, but at the time, I was neither keen on nor confident about it; a couple of my teachers had told me I was not good at math, and I believed it. The math department was notorious for being very hard—they never curved any tests, it took seven or eight years to graduate. I fully believed I would fail a lot and told my parents to get ready for it. As it turned out, I passed all my classes, graduating in three-and-a-half years! More importantly, I was actually not bad at math at all when taught in a deeper way, rather than "doesn't matter why, that's how it is," or "just memorize it."

Excited and pleasantly surprised about my newfound ability, at first, I focused on pure mathematics, without thinking about applications. After a few years, I found myself feeling that I wanted to study something else, although I didn't know exactly what. I would eventually find my way to the highly interdisciplinary field of cognitive science, the scientific study of the mind and cognition, and an area of science I didn't even know existed! Perhaps having read very widely from a young age—including my parents' books and textbooks, my mother's in psychology, my father's in science and engineering—contributed to my attraction to the field, but I was captivated and wanted to pursue it.

Starting from a pure mathematics background, it occurred to me that computer science could be a good entry point or transition towards cognitive science. I applied to a prestigious computer science department, where I obtained a Master's degree, focusing on artificial intelligence. I wrote my thesis on the Turing Test, which is about how to assess machine intelligence. Despite some challenges, I did very well, and having ascertained that I enjoyed research at the graduate level, I decided to apply for a Ph.D.

I was not sure I could gain admission to many graduate programs, having no formal biology or psychology background. I think I applied to seventeen different programs in cognitive science, computer science, neuroscience and psychology departments. I ended up getting invited for interviews at all of them, visiting something like twelve schools in just over two weeks! I was accepted to all these graduate programs. But I had fallen in love with U.C. San Diego's cognitive science department. Even though they gave me the worst offer in terms of financial support, this is where I chose to go for my Ph.D. I guess you could say I made an emotional decision.

Once I moved to San Diego and started the graduate program, I was surrounded by people who seemed to know so much more than I did about human cognition and the brain. In some courses, everything was foreign; at times I had absolutely no idea what the professors were talking about. I was very worried I might fail out and have to go back home. Somehow, I not only survived, I became fascinated by the brain. I had assumed my research focus would be on computational aspects of cognitive science since I had no cognitive psychology or neuroscience background, but now I was not so sure. I remember discussing my research direction with my advisor at the end of my first year, saying, "It's crazy for me to switch from computer science to neuroscience. I can't do all this." And she said, "Of course you can!" It was by no means a trivial transition, but she was right. I could.

During my Ph.D., I became interested in how the brain attaches meaning to different stimuli such as sounds or gestures. I worked with patients who'd had strokes—a humbling experience that taught me how very different real life could be from textbooks. In parallel, I was also doing human neuroimaging. I had more than enough studies going on for my Ph.D., which was by then fully focused on cognitive neuroscience. One day, I got an email about a seminar on campus by a professor from Japan whose lab made very life-like robots, like androids. I wouldn't normally go to a robotics talk, but for some reason I went to this one, and I was mind-blown! He was showing these super human-like robots with realistic skin, teeth, eyelashes, etc. My research was focused at the time on the perception of human body movements. And here were these robots making body movements. After the talk, I introduced myself to the professor, and he suggested we meet for lunch. We had a great discussion; I wrote a small grant for funding, which was successful. I went to Japan for a month, to videotape these human-like robots, so that we could study people watching them. My main interest was studying the brain, but this work also was related to my earlier research in artificial intelligence.

This interdisciplinary work not only opened up a new line of research for me, but also led me to fall into the "Uncanny Valley." The Uncanny Valley is about what happens when you make a robot (or an avatar or an animated character) very human-like, but not perfectly so. The idea is that some humanlike-ness is a good thing—e.g., an industrial robot may not be very engaging for a social application domain. But if we get really close to human appearance, things can instead get creepy. These agents can feel eerie or "zombie-like." Our studies indicate the Uncanny Valley may occur due to a mismatch

of features. Unless an agent's humanlike appearance is matched by humanlike behaviors (including natural bodily movements), the agent can evoke a negative response.

In sum, within the broad, interdisciplinary field of cognitive science, I studied artificial intelligence before transitioning to human cognitive neuroscience. Later, the robotics collaboration connected these two interests and lines of research. So now, I do all of the above. We use experimental studies with humans, different kinds of neuroimaging, and computational modeling to study both the human brain and human-robot interactions. It's fascinating work with many unknowns, and it keeps us busy!

Us: Of the book's themes, you embody "intelligence." Can you tell us what life experiences occurred to get you to embrace your intelligence?

A: It was at times difficult, to be honest, although I realized most of that in retrospect. At first, I didn't realize or even think about it. Part of the message may have come from my parents, and part from society in general, but showing off or making a display of one's intelligence was considered inappropriate, even arrogant, especially for girls. I was also not an attention-seeking child in general.

During my childhood, we had a summer house, where I spent most of my summers. I had a different friend group there than the rest of the year. When I was about ten or eleven, we were all into making friendship bracelets out of string. The bracelets would typically have colored stripes, slanting to the left or to the right. I figured out the geometry of how to make more complex designs with diamond shapes, and since I am fairly ambidextrous, I could change the direction of the knots without difficulty. When the other kids saw the bracelets I made with these complex designs, they wanted to know how I could do that. I gladly explained the logic behind how to combine the knots, and I helped those who wanted to try it. Naturally, I received more attention that day than usual. There was a girl a couple of years older, who was my friend. As I was helping those who wanted to make their own diamond patterned bracelets, I noticed her watching with this seething look in her eyes, which I didn't understand in that moment, but have never forgotten.

That evening, I walked down the hill to join my friends as I always did—but everything was different. I was ambushed by a group of my friends, upset and angry. After I tried to respond a couple of times, I quickly understood that the narrative against me was vague, incoherent, and untrue, but that didn't matter. The commotion turned into a literal witch-hunt, people calling me names like devil and demon. They were hurling insults, even throwing stones and spitting on me! In the midst of all this, I noticed the older girl, standing with her arms crossed, watching everything, smirking. At the time, I was confused how something like this—getting attention one day for making more unusual and elaborate friendship bracelets—could lead to this. A smart girl can be a very threatening thing.

Another incident of unwanted attention happened at elementary school. Everyone had to pass an exam to test their abilities in the English language before moving on to middle school. As a voracious reader, I had finished all the books in Turkish that we had at home and had started reading novels in English. As a result, my English was pretty advanced for my age. Still, my parents believed I could fail the exam and hired a tutor for me, a neighbor who was an English teacher at another school. She sent me home after ten minutes, saying I didn't need any tutoring. I remember my mother was shocked and called the woman to ask her to reconsider. I took the exam and scored first out of about 700 students. When this was announced, other students, who had been working hard all year for this exam, were crying. Apparently, coming first in this exam, along with perfect grades (which in elementary school a lot of people had), made me valedictorian. I hadn't even known that this was a thing—my parents even thought I might fail—but now I was thrown into the limelight. At our graduation, I not only had to give a speech in front of thousands of people, but I was set on a huge throne-like chair on the stage for the full three hours. You couldn't miss me if you tried!

At school the following year, everyone knew who I was and the bullying began. Everyone started calling me "nerd." After a while, I began intentionally to do less well in my school work than I was capable of. I also started acting out and being rebellious. I didn't want to be known as a nerd, although in the back of my mind, I also never let go of the desire to become a scientist. I was intentionally getting only so-so grades through middle and high school, but I knew that didn't really matter as long as I did well on the university entrance exam.

These are just a couple of stories from my childhood. I became more comfortable with being known as smart during college, but it wasn't until much later, towards the end of graduate school, that I found myself able to wholeheartedly embrace my intelligence as a positive.

Us: Successful people often get the "What is your greatest advice" question. We're asking it too! What is your best advice for girls and young women?

A: Trust your brain. So much happens unconsciously. The conscious you is only one part of you. Sometimes there are conflicting parts of you that want different things. This can explain why sometimes you think you want one thing, but you behave in a way that isn't consistent with that. So it's important to recognize that this is going on. Sometimes people express this idea as trusting your intuition, but that is actually not quite the same thing. Don't make rash decisions, but pay attention to yourself. If you notice something that persists in yourself over a long period of time, your brain may be telling you something important.

Us: What do you wish you had known earlier in your life that would have made your journey easier?

A: I wish that I hadn't believed the voices telling me that all the things about me that were "too much"—intensity of interests and emotion, passion, intelligence, or even style—were things to be ashamed of. Also, I wish I had understood the role of fear.

Sometimes, you don't understand why someone (including yourself) is thinking or behaving a certain way; you'd be surprised how often asking the question, "What are they afraid of?" gets you closer to the answer, or at least reveals some insight. People can be afraid of you; they can be afraid of themselves. They can be afraid of success as much as they are afraid of failure, sometimes simultaneously . . . Fear is complicated, not always conscious, and often not straightforward. It's also ever present. Then, I worried about my body, my weight, for far too many years. I was not someone who defined myself primarily on looks, yet like so many others, I struggled with an eating disorder. Then again, it never was about being attractive to others; it wasn't even about weight. It was only in my mid-twenties, when I suddenly found myself facing disability and a lifetime of (sometimes debilitating) chronic pain that I could finally shake myself out of that way of thinking. I find it sad how, for so much of my youth, every wish I made was about my weight. Alas, I cannot go back and enjoy my able and pain-free body now. So, as trite as it may sound to most young people, appreciating what we have, above all our health, is very important. Finally, a small thing: a good hairdryer and using a satin pillowcase saves so much time dealing with your hair!

Photo courtesy of Ayse Saygin

Us: What do you feel are the biggest obstacles that young women today have to face? How do you perceive most young women reacting to those obstacles?

A: Our nature is that of social primates. Humans are not solitary creatures. It is so built into us that even viewing a face on a screen activates social mechanisms in our brain. This may have a particularly confusing effect in today's environment, with technology from social media to robots and virtual reality increasingly part of our social lives. When you are young, you are trying to understand yourself, and yourself in relation to others. Young people today are potentially influenced by nearly everybody, with YouTube, Instagram, and so on. It's great that these things can allow us to connect with others and form community, but the other side is that you can be bombarded with input. And a lot of the social media that girls engage in can focus on appearance, make-up, fashion, fitness . . . Even if these aspects are not explicit, they can affect development and self-esteem, especially during adolescence and young adulthood. And, in parallel, people are also interacting less in person. Our brains evolved in a very different environment and haven't changed much from even thousands of years ago. This is all very new and we don't yet know how it's going to work out. It's not necessarily all a bad thing; but it's an open question. I am certain that it's influencing us, though, and can have important impacts on human psyche.

I worry about the idea that the time for feminism is over, that the fight has been "won," the playing field is now more or less equal, or even that it's gone too far. I worry that young women might themselves believe that—even I did, to some extent. Also, most people are not taking into account or even know of the role of unconscious biases. It's important for young women not to believe everything they hear, not take things as given, but to do their own research.

Us: What important character traits came most naturally to you, and which took longest to develop?

A: It took me a long time to value the right things, such as kindness, which I think may actually be the most important trait in humans . . . I was never unkind myself, except sometimes toward myself. But there was a time when I valued other things more, like whether someone knows advanced math and physics. I actually believed this! But that's silly, because who cares if you can triple integrate if you are not a kind person.

Seeing patterns came easily to me. In events, in people's behavior . . . or, like the diamond in the friendship bracelet, I suppose.

Us: Growing into a young woman, what influences were most liberating?

A: When I was young, I had a very un-gendered sense of myself and my abilities. And when I look back, I think this turned out to be liberating. If you construe yourself as one sort of thing, you start implicitly absorbing stereotypes about that thing. So, if I consider female—or say, athlete or scientist, doesn't have to be gender—as a primary part of my identity, then that affects me and how the world reacts to me. I didn't identify very much with societal ideas or messages about being female or male. I think that openness helped me have more diverse friends, and to draw inspiration more broadly. Carl Sagan, and his show Cosmos, for example, really cemented my desire to become a scientist. I knew of and admired Marie Curie, of course, but there really weren't that many famous female scientists. I think feeling open to be inspired by anyone, male or female, helped me.

Of course, I was never completely free of gender—I don't think that's realistic—but I think this continued to play a role later in my life as well. When I look at my colleagues, when they entered relationships or made plans to start families, it's almost always women who put their careers to the side, or at least curbed their ambitions. I'm not saying this isn't important or even necessary at times. But why should it be women making most of the room for these things? I know there are exceptions, but I don't see men doing it in academia. I never put my relationships ahead of my career-related decisions, and I think it was partly because I wasn't totally on board with the societal expectation that women are the ones who are supposed to do that.

Us: How do you know when you're on track, centered, or moving along your best path?

A: You have to look at your life as a whole. Consider not just work or whatever you're focused on. Your health, your relationships, your work . . . it's a lot to balance and it's not easy. It's a struggle, and in any of these areas you can get blocked. For example, if my work is going well and I am eating well and getting enough sleep, I probably have a month of laundry piled up. And maybe that's okay sometimes! But if your health or relationships are suffering, you may have to assess things and maybe make some changes. I think you can't assess how you are doing by looking at just one area.

Us: What's the hardest decision you made right?

A: I'm not sure. Maybe choosing where I went for my Ph.D.? Honestly, I feel like maybe it's something that hasn't happened yet.

Us: What do you do or what do you tell yourself when you have moments of self-doubt?

A: I try not to make major or binding decisions when I am going through hard times. Or even when I am emotional, tired, or sleep-deprived. I remember at one point in my post-doc, I was in Japan, severely jet-lagged and covered in mosquito bites. I'm allergic to mosquito bites, so I had these angry welts. I was exhausted but couldn't sleep. I was miserable. In that moment, in the middle of the night, I was so sure that I was on the wrong path in life and in my career. And just a couple days later, I recalled that moment and asked myself "What was wrong with you?" Just a small example.

Us: To which of your own values do you attribute your success?

A: In my field, and probably in general, once you get to a certain point, everyone around you is smart. Everyone is hard-working. Often, success comes through persistence. There have been plenty of times when I was discouraged or even treated unfairly—by peers, by colleagues, by my own health. . . . Learning to pick yourself up and keep going is crucial. Also, learning to control my rebellion. You don't have to buy into the game, but you have to learn to play it just enough. Sometimes, you have to play by the rules to survive in the system. Once you do, you have the opportunity to change it. Learning to manage my rebellion whilst keeping my integrity has been very important for me.

Us: How much of your success do you sense derives from your own values and actions as opposed to external factors?

A: There are some things I feel like I've done wholly from within myself. In the early stages of my chronic pain condition, my tendency was not to walk because it hurt so much. It was not even expected for me to be able to walk normally again. But having read about the condition, I forced myself to walk every day through the pain, which in the long term allowed me to have more mobility and less dystrophy than I would otherwise have had. But few things in life are based on your effort alone. For most things, certainly in my work, it's really a combination of what you put in and the people you are working with, and some luck! Remember, we are social primates. Sometimes you can't solve a problem just sitting around working on it by yourself. So I would say whatever success I've had was due to a combination of my own values and external factors.

Us: Thank you, Ayse!

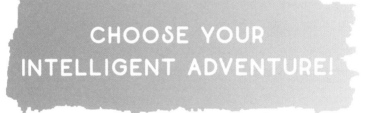

## CHOOSE YOUR INTELLIGENT ADVENTURE!

## *W*ALKABOUT 1:
### PHONEWORK

We understand the importance of smartphones. We rely on our cell phones for so much. But are you truly aware of just how often you pick up your phone and check it? Do you even know why you pick it up as often as you do? Understanding our behavior is very large part of being intelligent. If you do this next activity for just one single day, we promise you, the results will be mind-blowing.

**Get a pack of sticky notes. On as many sticky notes as you can, write just one word on each note:**

- Boredom
- Insecurity
- Curiosity
- Connection
- Necessity
- Loneliness

Now—and this is going to take practice and discipline—every single time you check your phone you must tear out one of your sticky notes and place it on the back of the phone. For example, if you picked up your phone because you were bored, you would tear out a sticky that has the word boredom on it. And so on. This seems simple, but can actually be a bit tricky. For example, if your check your texts on your phone because you want to know whether a potential significant other has responded to you, you might say that you were driven to do so by "curiosity". But what prompted the curiosity? Perhaps "insecurity", "connection" or "loneliness" are more appropriate choices here.

At the end of the day, tally up all your notes. How many in total? How many of each word? This activity isn't meant to make you feel bad. It's meant for you to understand your own behavior. When we know why we do the things we do, we are in a place to be able to take more control of our actions. And that makes you more intelligent.

# ✎*WALKABOUT 2:*
## MULTIPLE INTELLIGENCE

You've already read about the difference between book smarts and intelligence. In what ways are you intelligent that have nothing to do with book smarts?

 Circle all that apply to you. Add your own strengths if we missed some.

Circle all that apply to you & add your own if we missed some.

MOVEMENT / ATHLETICS

READING OTHER PEOPLE

MAKING FRIENDS

COOKING

ORGANIZING

EMPATHY

COMPASSION

UNDERSTANDING YOURSELF

MUSIC

PERCEIVING SUBTLETIES

CULTURAL AWARENESS

OPEN-MINDEDNESS

HUMOR

CURRENT EVENTS

ART

OTHER _____

MULTIPLE INTELLIGENCE

# WALKABOUT 3:
## DON'T BELIEVE THE MESSENGER

We already know that advertising agencies, news outlets, Hollywood, and social media send us messages all day long. We already understand that many of these messages are designed to prompt insecurities. (Look at all the "Before and After" photos—we're meant to judge others, and to compare ourselves.) We are so saturated with these messages that we barely notice the profound impact they have on our self-image.

**Let's do a field study. For the next week, pay careful attention to the myriad ways our judgement is assaulted by the different media in our lives. There is no such thing as getting too specific!**

How does media dumb us down?

What does media tell us about a woman's image?

What stereotypes are being sold to young women?

What does media teach about a woman's sexuality?

Which personal insecurities does advertising prey on?

How are women, including women of color, portrayed on TV?

Who do you see portrayed on TV in positions of power and excellence?

What career and educational status are women representing on scripted or reality shows?

What ideas about women do social media influencers produce?

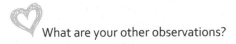 What messages on social media do you and your friends co-create about the value of being a woman?

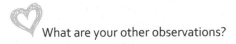 Who are the people behind media that produce these images of women? Do you believe their representation of women is complete and detailed, two-dimensional and incomplete, or somewhere in between? What are the driving forces behind their messages?

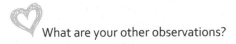 What are your other observations?

# $\mathcal{W}ALKABOUT$ 4:
## PERSONAL RETREAT

**Create a half day retreat for yourself.**

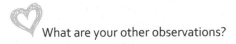 Parameters: Decide the timeline for your personal retreat. Set aside a minimum of two hours for yourself, and as much as a five-hour day. Tell the people you live with and other loved ones that you will be spending this time in silence. Prepare your meals in advance. Make a commitment to turn off all screens, not to read any books or magazines, and not to journal. This personal retreat is an opportunity for you to be with yourself and observe your own mind.

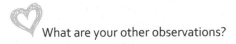 Begin the day by setting an intention to contemplate your own mind with a friendly curiosity. You can bring friendliness to your awareness by remembering to breathe, smiling at your thoughts, or consciously validating your feelings.

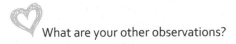 Humans have 50,000-60,000 thoughts per day. This time in silence is a chance to observe the web of thoughts that occupy your attention and your subconscious. You can stay seated, stretch, walk slowly, or even lie down (just don't fall asleep!).

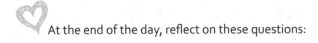 At the end of the day, reflect on these questions:

What did you observe about your mind?




Did you experience contradictory thoughts?




Where do thoughts come from? What determines
which thoughts become conscious and which remain
unconscious?

How seriously should you take all your thoughts?

To close the day, set an intention. How can you incorporate this experience of friendly observation into your everyday life?

YOUR PRIVATE PLACE FOR
NOTES OR DOODLES

You are more than your successes and failures. More than your accomplishments and fears. More than your perceived power and weaknesses. So far, far more.

Photo credit: Danielle Trina Photography

"The Warrior learns lasting lessons from the wealth of her life stories. She uses those lessons to guide her actions."

# WONDERFULLY WISE

## *Words about Wisdom from Those Who Have Gone Before You*

There are people who argue with great passion about how many stories exist. Most participants in these arguments quibble over whether the number is seven or eight. Some say the number is thirty-six. A few claim the number is as low as three.

What the story-number-arguers are talking about is the number of *essential* stories, the skeletal arrangements of plot and theme that lie at the heart of all storytelling. Infinite, unique variations on these essential stories can be created by rearranging and combining parts, and by introducing new details. It's similar to the idea that no two trees are alike, but that any tree is recognizably different from any rhinoceros.

(No two rhinoceroses are alike either, by the way.)

*Wait . . . but we are all different, so everybody's story is different . . . isn't my story unique?*

Yes, of course. It's possible for the two things to be true at once: everyone can own a unique story, and there can be a limited, and small, number of stories. That right there is a bit of wisdom!

Sometimes, especially among the young, the idea that in some sense we are all very similar, and we live out a limited number of stories, can feel insulting, restricting, or even frightening. The concept clashes with our sense of glorious individuality and threatens the possibility that anything we experience is truly new. Suddenly our universe has shrunk.

But it hasn't. Why not?

Well, for one thing, the universe itself is composed of a very small number of essential elements, all of them doing very simple things like attracting or repelling one another. But the universe still contains a pretty respectable amount of variety, wouldn't you say?

Let's take one example of an essential story, one that most of the arguers include in their arguments: The Voyage and Return. In this story, the main character travels to an unfamiliar place, overcomes obstacles and returns to the place they started, having learned something. This story is at the core of both *Goldilocks and the Three Bears* and *The Lord of the Rings*. Now, ask yourself a question:

At any point, as you watched (or read) *Lord of the Rings*, did you say to yourself, "Oh, this is basically just Goldilocks"? If not, then you'll understand why the concept of an essential story is no threat to your uniqueness. Your path is still your own!

By embracing the notion of the essential story, the idea that most behaviors, events, histories, phenomena, emotional journeys—or anything else we can experience or observe—boil down to a limited number of basic patterns, we arm ourselves to understand the world. And to understand ourselves.

In your mind, visualize a scene from a little play. An elderly woman sits on a park bench, hair in braids, cane in hand, a mysterious scar across her cheek. Next to her sits a young girl of seven or eight. The girl's face is lit with excitement and her entire body squirms with the emotion that underlies what she's saying to the woman. She's describing some dramatic experience from her young life. In other words, the little girl is telling the old woman a story.

Now, what does the old woman do? She listens. But how does she listen? She remains mostly still—the girl is animated enough for the both of them. She wears a gentle smile, colored with amusement, affection, perhaps the occasional note of concern. Mostly, she nods. She nods in recognition. She knows this story. She's heard it told a thousand ways by a thousand voices in a thousand places. She's lived this story herself. She knows how it ends, what other stories it leads to, and how all those stories can add up to a life. Knowing all this, two things are true of the elderly woman on the bench with the girl:

First, in a way that the little girl cannot, the old woman knows that everything will work itself out. The little girl will be fine. She will make the world into her playground.

Second, the elderly woman is delighted. The story she hears is as old as humanity, and endlessly repeated. But it is also new, and unique, and who knows how it will end?

Wisdom is the ability to see essential stories at work within the chaos of the world. It allows the Warrior to see herself in others, and to make deeply knowing decisions.

Wisdom grows in time—but not automatically. Wisdom needs experience, as much as it can get, which also means that wisdom needs failure. Warriors stand proud, supported by the wisdom of countless stumbles and painful falls.

Now go. See, do, fail and learn. Learn to tell your trees from your rhinoceroses.

THE NAKED TRUTH
with Dr. M. Lia Palomba,
Hematologist-oncologist,
specializing in the study and
treatment of lymphoma,
Memorial Sloan Kettering
Cancer Center

Photo courtesy of Dr. M. Lia Palomba

Us: Thank you for this interview, Dr. Palomba.

L: You're welcome.

Us: Ready to start?

L: Yes I am.

Us: Please tell us a little about yourself.

L: I am an Italian doctor who arrived in the United States to do research after I finished medical school in the late 1980s. I come from a very small island in Italy called Sardinia. Life there was very provincial and quite slow. I needed to expand my vision of the world, so I moved to a place south of Milan. It was very difficult for my parents to let me go. I was the only person leaving Sardinia. Believe it or not, everyone I know is still there. Nobody ever leaves! My parents and family expected me to stay in Sardinia. It was considered disrespectful to leave your family. It was very hard for all of us.

I had the opportunity to do research in the United States, so I moved here. It was such a big unknown in the beginning. There were no jobs because there were just so many doctors graduating from medical school. I met my husband and we built a life here in the United States. It was challenging to be a foreign woman and do the same job as a man here in the States. My husband and I started working at the same time, but I was about ten years behind in my training. I literally had to retrain to be able to work here. Eventually, we both found a place at the Cancer Center. But trust me, it was very hard.

Us: Successful women often get the "What is your greatest advice" question. We're asking it too. What is your greatest advice for young women?

L: Young women feel that they need to be beautiful and sexy, and in the end that is so completely irrelevant! Girls do not need to dress for boys! They need to focus on being creative and beautiful for themselves. It's also very important for young women to get the same level of education as men. Men seem to achieve more because women are often the ones doing the child rearing. If you want to succeed, go and get that degree. Do just as well, if not better than the guys. The hardest challenge for women is their lack of self-confidence. Many women just don't believe that they can achieve as much as men. Girls should pursue whatever they want, just like men.

Photo courtesy of Dr. M. Lia Palomba

Us: What to you wish you had known earlier in your life that would have made your journey easier?

L: I wish I had known that having family around me is much more important than I originally thought. Like I said earlier, I left them, thinking it was the right thing to do. Now, well, I realize how important they are and I miss them. I don't think anything could have happened earlier to make my life easier, actually. I needed to learn that on my own, and in my own time and way. Which is often the case for important insights.

Us: What do you feel are the biggest obstacles that young women today have to face?

L: There are no obstacles! Obstacles are created by peers and peer pressure. They are created by the culture in which she is growing up. School, social media. But, ultimately, there are no obstacles unless you create them yourself!

Us: What important character traits came most naturally to you, and which took longest to develop?

L: Honesty is part of my character. You will always know what I think of you. I'm also pretty generous. What took longer to develop was to learn not to over-react and not be impulsive. I'm still learning that trait. Probably always will be learning that.

Us: Growing into a young woman, what influences constrained you most, and what influences were most liberating?

L: I come from a very conservative family. I have three brothers. My mother was a strong woman and doctor herself, and she was a big role model for me. But when I finished high school, I wanted to become an architect. My parents refused to let me leave and go to college. When I insisted on leaving for medical school, it was really tough on them and it was hard for them to let me go. They eventually accepted what type of person I was. I think it was hardest for my father. He really struggled.

Us: How do you know when you're on track, centered, or moving along your best path? How do you know when you aren't?

L: I know that I am on track when I am happy with what I am doing. I don't do a lot that is boring, or that I don't care about. It's important to do things that you really like to do. When you are happy, happiness comes back to you. When I'm not on track, my interpersonal relationships suffer. All of my relationships, the ones with my family, colleagues, friends. It's not good. I can get negative. I can get depressed. And when this happens it interferes with all of life, and especially what I am working on.

Us: What's the hardest decision you made right? What's the easiest decision you made wrong?

L: Hardest decision I made right? Life is complicated. No clue.

Us: What do you do or tell yourself when you have moments of self-doubt?

L: I have people around who remind me when I get like this. I doubt myself too often. It's a daily thing for me. I have a tendency to be a bit depressed naturally. I think daily self-doubt is necessary. People who don't self-doubt are arrogant. I despise the people who don't have self-introspection. It's important that young women know there will be moments of doubt, and it's normal and healthy. It resets you.

Us: To which of your own values do you attribute your success?.

L: Perseverance. Not giving up.

Us: Thank you, Dr. P!

## WALKABOUT 1:
### PERSPECTIVE

Warrior, take a moment and tune in. Think of a current situation that is causing you discomfort or tension. Allow yourself to sense those feelings fully by breathing them in and letting them just be there. Don't think about fixing anything. After a few moments, start to picture yourself as an eighty-year-old looking back on this situation. What advice would she give you about your current predicament? Listen to her.

When we're in the middle of a troubling situation, our vantage point becomes narrow. But imagining yourself as possessing the gifts of time and experience opens up your energy. It helps you make decisions using wisdom that is actually already there, inside yourself.

```
What advice did your eighty-year-old self give
you?
```

# WALKABOUT 2:
## MEANING MAKING

Let's take a beat. Think of a mistake you've recently made. Let's go with a normal-size mistake, not the biggest one you've ever made, please. It could be an error as common as blurting out an insensitive remark or not remembering an assignment. Let the memory surface. Where were you? Who were you with? What went down? Allow yourself to feel the emotions of that human error. What did the mistake teach you?

Take three breaths.

Now, imagine that same scene. Where were you? Who were you with? Only this time, imagine yourself correcting the mistake. What are you doing differently? Take a moment and see yourself making a more beneficial choice. Notice how that feels and savor it.

```
Observations about how it feels to imagine correcting
my mistake:
```

When you're ready, bring your attention back into the present moment.

Warrior, you will make mistakes along the way, maybe even as soon as a moment from now. The next time that happens, remember that this is all learning. Okay, so you made a mistake. Be honest about it. Reflect on what you commit to do differently next time. Keep moving forward.

# WALKABOUT 3:
## MIRRORS

We become like the five people we spend the most time with. We can't help it. Our brains have mirror neurons, and we reflect the people who are in our lives.

Think of the five people you spend the most time with. What do they bring out in you?

How does your awareness of relationship mirrors help you on your quest as a Wanderlust Warrior?

# WALKABOUT 4:
## WISDOM PEDIGREE

Call to mind a story of a wise teacher in your life (professor, self-help guru, ancestor, fictional character, etc.) that speaks to you. What is it about their story that reaches your heart? How is it relevant to your life today?

Observations about my wise teachers:

In difficult moments, we can call upon our teachers and *their* teachers to lend us their wisdom.

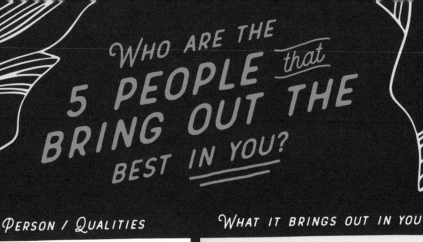

WHO ARE THE
5 PEOPLE *that*
BRING OUT THE
BEST IN YOU?

| PERSON / QUALITIES | WHAT IT BRINGS OUT IN YOU |
| --- | --- |
| | |
| | |
| | |
| | |
| | |

YOUR PRIVATE PLACE FOR
NOTES OR DOODLES

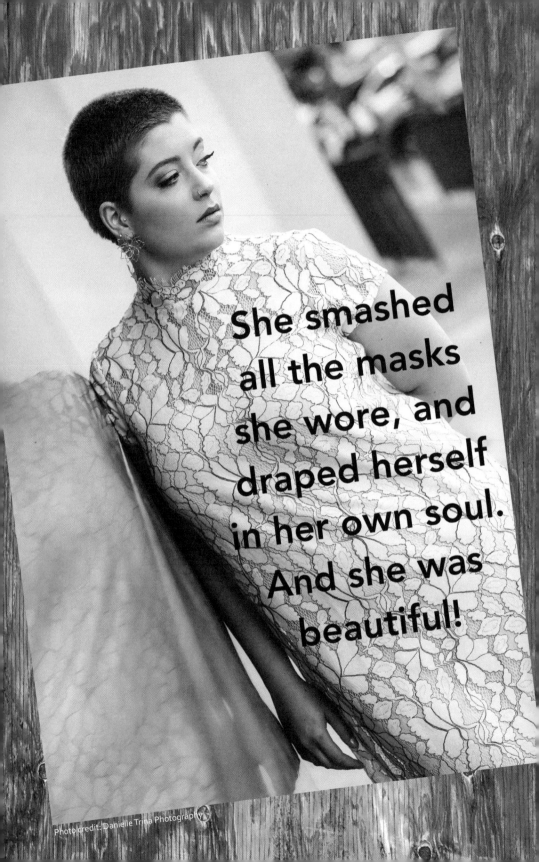

She smashed all the masks she wore, and draped herself in her own soul. And she was beautiful!

"The Warrior walks through the wilderness, braving the tang of fear, hearing its signals, and emerges her own heroic teacher."

# BE BOLD AND BRAVE

*Words about Bravery from Those Who Have Gone Before You*

Certain groups have popularized using "No Fear" as a mantra, a motto, or a declaration of some sort of powerful-sounding lifestyle.

That is utterly ridiculous, Warrior. Waste no time on such a childish idea.

There are, in fact, people who experience no fear. These are people who, usually because of a rare genetic disorder, experience catastrophic damage to a specific part of the brain. Their condition creates all sorts of problems in their lives. They display an extreme lack of self-control, often engaging in bizarre behavior that makes things like friendships, romantic relationships and employment exceptionally difficult. They find themselves in life-threatening situations with alarming frequency. In short, "No Fear" exists: as a life-wrecking mental disorder.

The Warrior knows fear. Intimately. She knows what fear feels like in her body and how it affects her mind. She knows its costs and its lessons. She values fear for the ways in which it serves her. And she works to overcome fear when it is time to act.

## Chapter 7

To be brave is to take important action despite the presence of fear. The greater the fear, the greater the bravery.

Take care to notice that not *all* action in the presence of fear is brave. It must be *important* action, in service of a worthy cause. To advance or protect something of true value.

Impulsive behavior, seeking an adrenaline high, is not brave. Often, it is foolish.

Overcoming fear to gain the admiration of others—such as making a grand display of a dangerous action—is not brave. It is weak.

Taking a great risk on the chance that it may result in a quick, easy gain is not brave. It is selfish and lazy.

You'll see that many behaviors masquerade as bravery, but something more common and less interesting lies beneath. Real bravery, true courage, is rare. Usually, it is quiet and humble. Often, it draws few admirers, and may even be scorned.

For the young, bravery that is scorned is the most difficult to master. Defending a bullied and unpopular peer, for example. Or, really, doing anything virtuous instead of something easier, sexier, or more accepted. The scorn that is likely to be heaped upon you turns one brave act into two—the brave act itself, and bravely withstanding the scorn.

For reasons like these, most brave acts go undone. In this way, bravery is like kindness—most kindnesses go ungiven. It is as easy to withhold bravery as it is to withhold kindness. But doing so comes at a cost to your own self-worth.

Each time you are confronted with the need to be brave, you've been presented with an opportunity. Take it, and you've written a proud chapter in your story—*no matter how things turn out*. Let it pass, and you've written a different kind of chapter. Even if nobody else seems to have noticed or seems to care, you will know. And you'll live with the chapter you've written.

Be kind to yourself, Warrior. Bravery is no easy thing. You won't always write the chapter you want to write. So be gentle—but expect a little more from yourself each day.

And leave the "No Fear" believers to their silly games.

## The Naked Truth

with Catt Sadler,
Former Entertainment Anchor/
Host at E! Entertainment,
Activist, Blogger

Us: Hi Catt! Thank you for this interview!

C: Happy to be here.
Us: Should we get right to it?

C: Yup. All set.

Us: Please tell us a little about yourself.

C: I am a journalist, activist, entrepreneur, tastemaker, and mother. I spent twenty years as an entertainment anchor/TV host on E!, but recently left over a wage gap issue.

Us: Of the book's themes, you embody "brave". Can you tell us about being brave?

C: I chose to leave my dream job when I determined I was being treated unfairly compared to my male counterpart. I worked longer hours, had more on-air time, had worked at the company for an equal amount of time, but was paid significantly less. I found the courage to stand up for myself and what was right. It was a very scary decision to make, because I had to think about the possible ramifications of leaving. Would I be able to financially support my two children in the future? Would there be professional repercussions from other employers in the industry, who might question my position? If I told my story publicly, would people criticize or question my motives, or would they support my stance?

Us: Successful women often get the "What is your greatest advice" question. We'll ask it too. What is your best advice for young women everywhere?

C: My biggest advice to young women everywhere is to be your authentic self, not a second-rate version of somebody else. The most successful people I know all have one thing in common: individuality. There is a supreme uniqueness to the way they think, the way they operate, the way they impact others. Learn to tap into your particular strengths and spend as much time as you can growing your gifts. Run your own race, don't spend your energy worrying about what others are doing. The most difficult part of doing this is that we often compare ourselves to others—what they're achieving, when they're achieving it. Do not get wrapped up in this. Stay the course. Learn your purpose and then keep your attention on all of the things you must do to bring it forth!

Us: What do you wish you had known earlier in your life that would have made your journey easier?

C: I wish I would have understood the power of networking. I simply believed in my abilities and assumed they would take me far. But had I cultivated a network of mentors and contacts, I think I could have climbed more quickly towards my dreams. Reach out to those whom you admire. Take risks, ask questions, work hard, work for free, write thank you notes, pay attention to the little things, care about others . . . this will all come back to you. In many ways, I think I'm introverted, even though what I do for a living requires a large personality. Don't play it safe in your bubble; cast a wide net on all that life has to offer and you'll be amazed at what comes back to you! I probably would have learned all of this earlier had I cultivated an intimate relationship with a superior or mentor early on in my career.

Us: What do you feel are the biggest obstacles that young women today have to face? How do you perceive most young women reacting to those obstacles?

C: I think, because of technology and everything being at our fingertips, everything seems impermanent in a way. It's tempting and too easy for girls to get lost online in a make-believe world that doesn't reflect real life. So many hours are wasted on this distraction, which also includes far too many opinions of others. My advice would be to unplug more, detach from social media as often as possible, surround yourself with like-minded friends who are idea makers, readers, dreamers. Cleanse yourself as often as possible from the noise that comes along with your handheld device! But don't get me wrong. Much of my business is monetizing my digital presence. It's a powerful form of media, but just be aware of the drawbacks!

Us: What important character traits came most naturally to you, and which took longest to develop?

C: I'm naturally curious about other humans, so I'm very inquisitive. That has helped me in storytelling. I'm respectful, energetic, organized and driven. It was harder for me to learn courage. I often only did things I was certain I could succeed at.

Us: Growing into a young woman, what influences constrained you most, and what influences were most liberating?

C: I was most constrained growing up by my peers and even elders in the small town in which I was raised. There was kind of this approach to life that was stunted. Limits on how much you could do or achieve. Big dreams were said to be just that—dreams. There were a few adults that were the exception, though. My drama teacher in high school, a few friends' parents, my college counselor . . . their support and encouragement helped open up so many possibilities for me! When I was about twenty, it finally dawned on me that the only limitations in life are the ones we put on ourselves.

Photo courtesy of Catt Sadler

Us: How do you know when you're on track, centered, or moving along your best path? How do you know when you aren't?

C: When I'm on my best path, everything is seemingly more effortless. I'm taking care of my mind, body and soul—yoga, eating clean, reading a lot—and, wouldn't you know it, everything just aligns better. Answers come to me more clearly, obstacles never seem too big, ideas flow out of me. I think we have to consistently nurture ourselves and practice self-care. When we do this, I truly believe there is this universal support guiding us toward our best lives. You can literally feel the difference. The opposite of this is constant chaos; illness; roadblocks; short, shallow stress breathing. Pay attention. The signs are always there.

Us: What's the hardest decision you made right? What's the easiest decision you made wrong?

C: The hardest decision I made right was walking away from my job after twelve years, going public and speaking my truth. The rewards have been endless and others' lives have been impacted positively.

Us: What do you do or tell yourself when you have moments of self-doubt?

C: I tell myself that *everyone* has self-doubt. I try to channel feelings of self-love and recall feelings when I've felt my best, strongest, most powerful self. Sometimes meditating on those moments or past accomplishments can help take negative thoughts away.

Us: To which of your own values do you attribute your success?

C: I think, in the world of TV journalism, having a relatable personality has served me, in a way. People have felt comfortable over the years watching me and are drawn to my authentic way of interviewing people. I think the audience appreciates it. And I think celebrities and high-profile public figures have naturally opened up more because of it. There's a real, non-threatening vibe about me that has been useful in these conversations.

Us: What else should we know about you?

C: I'm a Hoosier. I have two boys and we all love basketball. I have six tattoos. I love to sing and dance. I'm athletic. Stamping my passport is my favorite hobby. Traveling has changed my life!

I have a fashion, beauty, and lifestyle website: thecattwalk.com. I'm writing a book. I'm starting a podcast very soon and I'm selling a TV series as we speak—serving as executive producer alongside Jennifer Lawrence!

Us: You're awesome, Catt! Thank you!

# CHOOSE YOUR BRAVE ADVENTURE!

## *WALKABOUT 1:*
### OWN IT WHEN YOU BLOW IT

Do you ever find yourself apologizing for things that don't matter? The phrase "I'm sorry" becomes filler, a way to ease the awkwardness of empty space. When you pay attention to that habit, you'll see your reflex apology is coming from a feeling of insecurity. Or do you tend to go the reverse route, and avoid saying sorry when it's actually appropriate? Pride or fear might hold you back in those situations. But when you deny the apology, you miss out on repair and connection with the other and yourself.

**Before making an apology, ask yourself these four questions:**

- Do I need to take accountability for something?
- Will it help me repair the relationship?
- Will it support my personal growth?
- Would it be helpful to do an act of service to truly make amends?

"I'm sorry'" is only the first part of the journey. The next step is to make a genuine effort to change the behavior. That's what makes the apology count.

Is there anyone in your life to whom you need to make an apology? Talk with a mentor or someone you trust about the best way for you to make amends. It doesn't always require a face-to-face conversation.

Who is this person?

What do you need to apologize for?

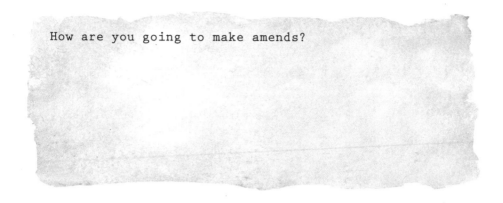

How are you going to make amends?

# WALKABOUT 2:
## DO THE SCARY

List five things that scare you. They can be small scary things, like asking a question in school or speaking up in a meeting. Even starting a conversation with someone you want to get to know better. They can also be big scary things, like jumping out of an airplane or going somewhere all alone.

Scary thing 1:

Scary thing 2:

Scary thing 3:

Scary thing 4:

Scary thing 5:

Now, pick one or all of your scary things and go do them. This Walkabout is not easy, Warrior. This Walkabout gets you out of your comfort zone. We suggest that you start with a small scary thing and work your way up. You may not even get to your biggest scary thing, and that's fine. The point here is to conquer some of the fear that you carry with you. Being brave is all about feeling the fear and doing something anyway. Being brave is not about not experiencing fear. Being brave is about action. Now, go take some action!

# *W*ALKABOUT 3:
## REACH OUT FOR IT

If you look back in history, the role of women has often been to wait. In prehistoric times, women would wait in their villages while men hunted prey for the winter months. During the Renaissance, ladies would bide their time as chivalrous knights proved their honor and won a woman's hand in marriage. In the 1950s, when social norms dictated that a woman's place was in the home, women were told how to pretty themselves or make a comfortable home while they waited for their men to get home from work. Today, women are still waiting—waiting for equal wages, waiting for equal opportunity, waiting to walk the earth with the sense of safety and privilege that our male counterparts take for granted.

Whether by society at large or members of our households, many of us have been conditioned to be "good girls" who don't challenge the status quo. We learn to become almost needless and wantless. This is the work of the patriarchy. As Warriors, we must become better friends to ourselves, be willing to acknowledge what we want, and then go after it. Reaching out for our wants and needs is an act that breaks generational patterns of hiding and passivity.

**Have you been waiting to . . .**

- Travel to a new spot?
- Go for your dream job?
- Ask for a raise?
- Ask your friend to stop doing something that hurts your feelings?
- Apply to the school of your highest choice?
- Pursue life as an artist?
- Start serving from your heart?
- Get sober?
- Ask your crush out on a date?

Wanderlust Warrior, take a leap! It doesn't matter how small or how big your desire; set your gaze on what you want and go for it. You may need to make preparations for the journey.

Map out your first three steps:

What is it that you want?

Who do you need to reach out to?

What actions are required of you?

## FOLLOW THROUGH!

What have you learned about yourself as you begin to reach out for your heart's desires?

What do you need to remember as you take your next steps?

How has reaching out changed your life?

# *W*ALKABOUT 4:
## EMBRACE THE MYSTERY

Do you ever find yourself obsessing over results? For instance, if you study really hard, you *must* get the "A"? If you were super nice to someone, they *should* like you? If you jumped through all the hoops, you *deserve* the prize?

The cold reality is that life doesn't always work this way. We don't always get the outcome we want. Facing this truth can make you feel scared and out of control. Not knowing how it's all going to turn out is difficult.

And yet . . .

Often it's the mystery or uncertainty in life that allows us to experience hope, excitement, anticipation, and even thrill. Sometimes the unknown is really where it's at.

Think of a time when you had to hang out in a state of uncertainty. Whether eventually you got what you wanted or not, what was it like to anticipate that thing? How did not knowing the result make you a stronger person? Even if you didn't get what you wanted, was it still worth taking the risk?

How does accepting the mystery make you a brave Warrior?

YOUR PRIVATE PLACE FOR
NOTES OR DOODLES

Honesty is what happens when you fall in love with the truth.

Photo credit: Danielle Trina Photography

"The Warrior accepts from herself and others no substitute for truth. She does not shrink from raw reality."

# HONESTLY, BE HONEST

### *Words about Honesty from Those Who Have Gone Before You*

So, there's you. And there's the rest of the universe . . . of which you're a part.

And within you, there are different parts. What you experience from one moment to the next is just the tip of a massive iceberg. Every sensation and conscious thought has been selected from countless others that also occupy your mind. Within your subconscious, many different voices clamor to be heard. Only a few make the cut and rise to the surface, where you can perceive them.

All these parts can work together, in alignment, or in opposition. The different parts of yourself can be on the same page, or at odds. And you can operate in alignment with what is outside of you, or you can pretend.

All of this goes to say that being honest is simply about getting all the parts yourself on the same page, and getting yourself as a whole on the same page with what seems actually to be true "out there".

Doing otherwise is a waste of your time.

You will fail to be honest. Frequently. When you fail, it will be to avoid some sort of pain. That's okay, as long as you notice what you've done, pin down why you've done it, and resolve to aim a bit higher as you travel the remainder of your path. Your moments of dishonesty offer valuable information about yourself, and shine light into your darker corners. Don't you want to know what's in there? Maybe make those corners a little less dark, a little less mysterious, a little less able to control you?

It is possible to travel the full length of your path without ever being completely honest with yourself. Many people do. Many good people, who do noble and important things, who love (as much as their dark corners allow them) and are loved. But, for these people, something is always not-quite right. They never reach the heights they otherwise might have—maybe they've persuaded themselves that they're not really capable, or that the world has conspired to hold them down. They do not love as they might have loved, and never feel completely seen and fully loved. They live as a shadow of themselves.

In truth, we all fit this description to some extent. Honesty is not a destination, some mountaintop that a heroic few have actually achieved. It is a process. A difficult one, with risks and rewards to match. The difference between the Warrior and those who have yet to become Warriors is that the Warrior sees this struggle to live honestly as the struggle it is, and then embraces the work.

Here's a tip to increase the chances you'll be honest when it really counts: expect yourself to crumble when faced with the temptation to lie, to yourself or to others. Knowing that you'll often stumble, create situations ahead of time that don't present you with the temptation. Invite others, people you trust, into your life. Open your books to them. Shine light on how you work, as a habit. This way, you'll make it more difficult for yourself to withdraw into the dark corners when it matters—those corners won't be there!

Over time, you'll acquire a taste for sunlight. You'll start to do the decent and difficult thing as a gift to yourself, because you know you'll be happier in the long run. You'll be less surprised and more compassionate when others haven't been honest with you. The chorus within you will make harmonious sounds—the soundtrack to your journey on the path.

THE NAKED TRUTH
with Nancy Gale,
Founder, Jamah Bags and
Founder, The Ambition Program

Photo courtesy of Nancy Gale

Us: Hi Nancy! Thanks for the interview!

N: It's my pleasure. I love what you're doing.

Us: Thank you! Ready to get started?

N: I'm all set and ready, yes.

Us: Please tell us a little about yourself.

N: I am a luxury handbag designer and own Jamah, an American luxury design house with all design and production hand-made in the U.S.A. I've also integrated a non-profit organization called Ambition. Ambition is an entrepreneurial program that focuses on solution-driven thinking and problem-solving for under-privileged youth. The two brands came together because I realized that I wanted a brand that really stood for something. Something that was really important to me. I grew up in Detroit, watching the auto industry diminish in Michigan. It had a huge impact on me. I realized that there were no real luxury design centers located in the U.S.A. We have a wealth of talented craftspeople here, but very few luxury artisans. . . I wanted the brand to represent luxury made here, but the other piece that really mattered to me was recognizing that I grew up with a lot of access and exposure. I wanted to share that with others who didn't really have that access and those resources.

There are so many people who grow up not just feeling like they can't be in the high-end retail world, but actually feeling shunned from that world. I wanted to create something that was a platform that . . . was about people seeing they could step forward and do. What I realized was that I wanted a brand and a non-profit that was based on resilience. Resilience has been the theme of my life.

My mother was very ill when I was young. She spent many years in the hospital . . . the majority of my high school years. She rallied through it all. But during that time, many folks and my dad spent a lot of time making sure my life was as normal as it could be. That experience really heightened my resilience. And made me realize that resilience is something we work towards, it's not really something we are born with. Events in my life prompted even more resilience. I was raped as a young adult, right after college. Again, my resilience kicked in. I made a lot of discoveries about my personality after that. The best process of healing for me was to be working with people who were in need. I began speaking with women at self-defense schools. I could talk about choices and decisions that I had made. So I became focused on how we own our actions. Not in a blaming way, but in the way that all our choices belong to us.

As I make all my choices now, it's interesting how I go to own something and people around me say things like, "You've been through some hard times, you can't blame yourself." It's when we start taking responsibility that there are mounds of people telling you not to! I find that odd.

In 2000, my father passed away. I was extremely close to him. It was an unspeakable death. When he passed, my resiliency really jumped in again and I realized that, other than missing him, I was okay. At that point, my business really started growing and I decided to take Jamah from a mainstream, moderate luxury line to a really high-end line, with the goal of having Jamah be the first true American luxury design house. I also formed Ambition at that time. And I combined the two in my head. When you buy a bag from Jamah, it allows us to give even more to the kids.

Photo courtesy of Nancy Gale

Then my mom was murdered. It was a home invasion. Resilience was truly tested once again. And it won. I respected the horrible pain, but instead of crumbling, I had to keep going. I had to keep running my business. It's been six years since then, and there are some things I wish I had handled differently. And, in my next challenging situation, I will be able to do that. My mother's case went cold. But we were diligent and disciplined and were able to get the case active again. There hasn't been one place in my career or life where it hasn't been about figuring it out and marching forward. No vision is too big.

Us: Successful women often get the "What is your greatest advice" question. We're asking it too! What's your best advice for young women?

N: My advice would be to know the core of your vision so well that you are able to differentiate the advice you are getting from people, so you can determine the amount of effort you should put into the advice you get. What's challenging is that, when you have an idea, once you get around people who are successful, it's easy to run away from your core. It's easy to believe that others know more than you. There is some great advice out there that will help you. The best way to know is to be really solid in your core. When you are hearing advice, listen to it all. And then go to another space where no one is around you and figure out what is applicable.

Us: What do you wish you had known earlier in your life that would have made your journey easier?

N: I wish I knew that, if I was talking to people who were more successful than me, that they were once in the same place I was. I wish I knew that those people were actually just people. We can get skittish around people who we think have achieved.

Us: What do you feel are the biggest obstacles that young women today have to face? How do you perceive most young women reacting to those obstacles?

N: The biggest obstacle is that there is so much information. We are almost having to figure out what we think and feel from . . . people around us. We stay in pack mentality. When I was growing up, there was a different sense of discovery. I'm not sure if this generation is making their decisions or establishing what they believe from their own core. They glom on to decisions instead of making their own. Ask yourself the question, why do I believe this, why do I think this way? Do you really believe what you think you believe?

Photo courtesy of Nancy Gale

Us: What important character traits came most naturally to you, and which took longest to develop?

N: Resiliency came early and naturally. Being happy in every situation, even when challenged and sad, comes easy to me. I'm still developing my public confidence. That said, sometimes [it comes naturally] and other times I want to sink into the woodwork. I continue to develop tools to work around that.

Us: Growing into a young woman, what influences constrained you most, and what influences were most liberating?

N: I've always had a big mind. I don't know if that is nature or nurture. Growing up, words and sentences I heard all the time were things like "That's great, but impossible. Too big, too much, you can't do that." Since I was a young girl, I recognized that the Wright brothers could get their machine to fly. I remove myself from situations where people believe those big things are for other people. It took me a long time to realize that it was impossible to *them*. Advice I wish I had learned . . . if someone can't imagine something for themselves, they can't imagine it for you.

Us: How do you know when you're on track, centered, or moving along your best path? How do you know when you aren't?

N: When I am on my path, my life is like an internal instrument . . . it all sounds right. I started sky diving and was pretty avid. Once I came out of the airplane, the person I was strapped to flew away from me. I opened my chute and felt empowerment. It's so amazing, all the pieces were in place. I set out to do something and I was jumping on my own! I looked down and thought, "This is the moment all the pieces are connecting, internally and externally." That feeling of connection has become my benchmark. When the inside matches the outside.

Same answer for the second part of the question. When the outside doesn't connect with inside, I need to stop. Turn off phone. Turn off world and sit. Like a machine. Reset myself.

Us: What's the hardest decision you made right? What's the easiest decision you made wrong?

N: The easiest decision I made wrong was looking for someone to replace the support I had received from my mom. I was looking for someone to have my back like she did. Any time someone seemed like they could bring something to my business, I jumped into a partnership. I did it four or five times to my detriment.

The hardest decision I made right was to stop going down that path.

Us: What do you do or tell yourself when you have moments of self-doubt?

N: I focus on the things that I have achieved. My greatest achievements. Some personal, some professional. Self-doubt is good if one takes a direction of being proactive, despite the doubt. I would call it self-assessment, and not self-doubt.

Us: To which of your own values do you attribute your success?

N: Resiliency and positivity.

Us: What else should we know about you?

N: If you have methodical discipline and follow-through, you'll reach success. . . . Have determination and really hone that skill. You can't just have a vision. You have to look at what it takes to enact that vison. It's also learning to discern who to share your goals and dreams with. Some people can pull you down.

Us: Thank you, Nancy!

## CHOOSE YOUR HONEST ADVENTURE!

### WALKABOUT 1:
#### LIAR, LIAR!

Think about the last time you lied to someone. It could have been a little white lie or the Grandmother of All Lies. Write it down here:

Usually we lie to protect ourselves or others from some form of emotional pain. Thinking about the lie that you told above, what do you think you were trying to protect yourself from? (If you had told the truth, then . . . what hurtful thing might have happened?) Were you protecting someone when you lied?

Now think of a time someone lied to you. Write it down.

What do you think they were trying to protect themselves from? Were they trying to protect you?

# WALKABOUT 2:
## WHAT'S YOUR DREAM?

We are all born with a dream, or a sense of what we are meant to do with the life we've been given. The dream may evolve a lot over time, but it usually keeps a constant, important theme. There is no dream too small or big, as long as it means something to you.

What is your dream for your life?

# WALKABOUT 3:
## ASK FOR HELP

One of the most difficult things to do is to look inward and admit a personal weakness. If this were easy, we'd all be doing it all the time. When we face our weak spots, we may find ourselves on a scary, lonely road. That's why asking trustworthy people in our lives for support is so helpful. We don't have to walk alone.

**Here are some common areas in which we can ask for help:**

"I have this pesky little habit of dating jerks. I'm over it. The next time I'm interested in someone, will you meet them and tell me what you really think?"

"I keep gossiping about people and I'm trying to stop. Can you help me stay more positive when we talk?"

"I've been beating myself up lately whenever I make mistakes. Will you remind me to be gentler with myself when I'm struggling?"

Is there a failing you can admit to yourself? Who can you ask to support you? How can they support you in your work to be more honest with yourself?

# $\mathcal{W}$ALKABOUT 4:
## THE TRAP OF SHOULDS

Have you ever fallen into "The Trap of Shoulds"? It's that deep pit of judgment, where we criticize others and ourselves for what we should or shouldn't be doing.

"She should not be wearing that."
"She should mind her own business."
"She shouldn't freak out like that."
"I should have studied longer."
"I should be a better daughter."
"I shouldn't have messaged him."

When we fall into The Trap, we are rejecting life as it is and trying to control our world. Yet, "shoulding" shrinks our powerful nature and limits our ability to accept life as it is.

The next time you get caught in The Trap, try looking deeper.

**Ask:**

 What is making me uncomfortable about this moment?

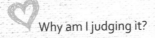 Why am I judging it?

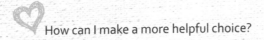 How can I make a more helpful choice?

Your willingness to look deeply and to tell the truth is your way through The Trap, to "The Path of Acceptance."

# $\mathcal{W}$ALKABOUT 5:
## THE PATH OF ACCEPTANCE

Living honestly means seeing our situation clearly. It doesn't mean we have to like it. It doesn't mean we support, condone, or sweep it under the rug. Paying attention and seeing something clearly removes our blind spots and helps us learn how to accept

"What Is." If we are ever able to change, it is because we have first accepted.

Try using "I See" mantras to build your practice of acceptance. Practice saying these things without labeling them as good or bad.

I see this family pattern:
I see this habit between me and my friends:
I see this quality in my significant other:
I see this part of my personality:
I see these dynamics at school:
I see this challenge on the job:
I see this issue in the world:

Use the I See mantra daily. Take notice of what it opens up for you.

## Bonus

### The Naked Truth
with Toni Ko,
Founder, NYX Cosmetics,
Founder, THOMAS JAMES LA
by PERVERSE sunglasses,
Founder, Toni Ko Foundation

Photo courtesy of Toni Ko

Us: Thank you so much for this interview!

T: I'm happy to part of what you are doing.

Us: Let's dig right in! Can you tell us a little about yourself?

140

T: I'm a serial entrepreneur. I have developed, launched, and built highly successful global brands. This past April, I launched my second company, THOMAS JAMES LA by PERVERSE sunglasses, after I recognized a gap in the accessories market between the expensive sunglass brands sold in department stores and the mass brands sold in retail stores. I designed the THOMAS JAMES LA collection for those with style and substance.

I founded my first company in 1999, at the age of twenty-five, the multi-million-dollar cosmetics brand NYX, which was acquired by L'Oreal in 2014. I created NYX with the goal of delivering professional, richly pigmented products at affordable prices. I worked as a one-woman show from a six hundred square foot show room in California, and I started with selling a single item—makeup pencils. I generated two million dollars in sales during the first year, and quickly grew to become a leader in the color cosmetics industry, gaining the respect of such retail giants as Target, CVS and Ulta.

I really credit my family as the primary influence on my education in the beauty business. I worked in the family-owned beauty supply store in Los Angeles, which my mother opened shortly after they immigrated from Korea when I was thirteen years old. I sold NYX to Loreal at forty-one years old, and it had revenue growth of well over one hundred million dollars.

It was a dream of mine last summer when I was on the cover of *Forbes* annual "America's Richest Self-Made Women" issue. Previously, I had been featured in several reputable publications, including *Entrepreneur, Inc. Magazine, The Los Angeles Times, Marie Claire*, and *Cosmopolitan*.

I have received numerous awards, including most recently being honored alongside Rachel Zoe, Abigail Breslin and Tracee Ellis Ross at the National Women's History Museum's "Women Making History" brunch. I was also named Entrepreneur of the Year from the Asian Business Association, received the 2015 Leadership Award from NAWBO, and the Lifetime Achievement Award by the Beauty Bus Foundation in 2013. Also in 2013, NYX was the WWD Beauty Inc. pick for Brand of the Year, which was one of the most defining moments in the industry.

I started the Toni Ko Foundation in 2014, where I lend support to organizations that help children in need and those that empower women. I discovered the majority of top executives are men, and I want to enable women with the courage to start their own businesses and set higher goals to be the executives. The only way for many women around the globe to be more liberated is to become financially independent. I think it's incredibly important to lead women in the right direction to achieve independence.

Us: One of many themes that seem important in your story is Persistence! Please tell us what life experiences occurred to get you to embrace your inner Persistence.

T: My experience as a thirteen-year-old who was plucked out of everything she had known in her life then moved and transplanted in another country. I had to learn a whole new culture and language. There are 7.6 billion people worldwide and 244 million are estimated to be immigrants/migrants living outside of the country they were born in. That's only about three percent of the entire world, and being one person out of that equation [is to] have experienced something very significant and special.

Us: Successful people often get the "What is your greatest advice" question. We'll ask it too.

T: There are so many great pieces of advice, but there is one that I received from another female entrepreneur whom I consider my mentor that I want to share: "Focus only on the goal. Everything else is just noise." It's extremely simple yet powerful. Those words helped me focus on the sale of my company while I was going through the transaction. Often times we get caught up with feeling and emotions. When doing business, it's a must to be able to turn off those emotions and focus only on the goal.

Us: What do you wish you had known earlier in your life that would have made your journey easier?

T: Know how and when to say "no." I had always been a "yes" person . . . I said "yes" to many commitments, to a point I was stretched too thin. In retrospect, now I realize how unhealthy over-commitment was both to my business and to my personal health. When you are over-committed you become tired, and when you are tired, it affects one's decision-making skills. I learned it's okay to not say "yes" to every function, event, meeting, request, ask, etc.

Us: What important character traits came most naturally to you, and which took longest to develop?

T: I had always been a doer since I was little. I wholeheartedly volunteered for all types of chores and whatnot. It made me happy making other people happy. I think this was crucial to my success. Often people say, "Nice people finish last," but I don't believe that one bit. All the highly successful—or at least the majority of highly successful people—I know are extremely kind people. This goes back to the earlier question, of learning to say "no." It was really hard for me to say no to people's requests because what made me happy was making others happy, and saying no [seemed] the exact opposite of that. It took me a very long time to realize that saying no does not make me a bad person, and that it was okay to say no.

Us: Growing into a young woman, what influences constrained you most, and what influences were most liberating?

T: Definitely my Korean culture constrained me the most. The Asian philosophy of being a socially conscious person is often different from the Western culture. For instance, I have extreme difficulty accepting compliments. Compliments make me uncomfortable. I know this sounds crazy, but this is an example of the philosophy difference. Where I grew up, [until you are] thirteen years old, if you accept a compliment then you are a vain person, because by saying "thank you" you are acknowledging that you are great. A proper way to intercept a compliment is to profusely rebut it. So when I came to the US and had someone give me a compliment, there I was, adamantly denying whatever I was being complimented for. Later I realized this was not only making the person uncomfortable, but was downright rude. This is just an example of many similar stories. And the most liberating experience (it's not an influence) was when I started my business and became financially independent. The only and the truest form of independence is to be able to support yourself.

Photo courtesy of Toni Ko

Us: How do you know when you're on track, centered, or moving along your best path? How do you know when you aren't?

T: I believe the most effective way to determine this is to listen to what your gut tells you. As women, we all have a sixth sense. If your instinct tells you it's wrong, it probably is, and vice versa. All these years as an entrepreneur and an independent woman, one thing I can be sure of is that my instincts are often times better than data or spreadsheets.

Us: What's the hardest decision you made right? What's the easiest decision you made wrong?

T: The hardest decision I made right was selecting the right company to acquire my company, NYX Cosmetics. I was offered many options, but I always knew L'oreal would be the best custodian of something I loved dearly . . . Building NYX brand for almost fifteen years was everything I had and known in most of my adult life, and I wanted the next owner of this brand to be able to build NYX into a true global brand which L'oreal did. I am so proud to see NYX stores all over the world. I was in Bordeaux in August and came across a NYX store. The butterfly I feel in my stomach every time I see one abroad cannot be described. It feels like falling in love over and over again. The easiest decision I made wrong was selling the company slightly prematurely. I am not the person to regret my decisions but this one may be one exception. I actually wanted to pull out of the deal and run the company for a couple more years, but eventually I made the final decision to go ahead with the acquisition. We were too deep in to pull out without pissing off some people. Hindsight, it would actually have benefited everyone involved if we held the company for a couple more years. But let bygones be bygones and move on, move forward!

Us: What do you do or tell yourself when you have moments of self-doubt?

T: I have self-doubts all the time. I think it's a natural human feeling. My father taught me this which I use all the time. Say to yourself, "I can do this" and repeat ten times.

Us: To which of your own values do you attribute your success?

T: I value being a value-add to the society I belong to and to people around me. I think that's my value.

Us: How much of your success do you sense derives from your own values and actions as opposed to external factors?

T: All of it. My goal in life is to not be a burden but adding value to anyone or anything around me. So I act with this internal value. This is a highly effective way to motivate one's self. And motivation leads to results.

Us: Thank you, Toni!

T: It was my pleasure.

*Your Private Place for Notes or Doodles*

The fact that you don't know what's right over that wall is the whole point. Stay curious, Warrior, and start climbing!

Photo credit: Danielle Trina Photography

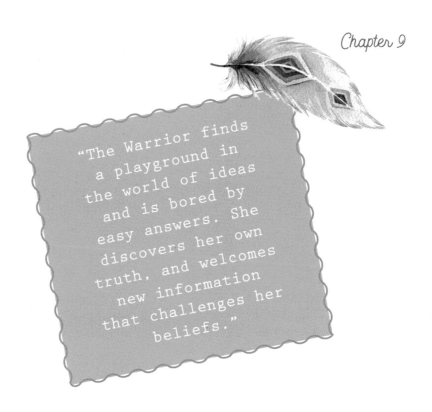

"The Warrior finds a playground in the world of ideas and is bored by easy answers. She discovers her own truth, and welcomes new information that challenges her beliefs."

# CULTIVATE YOUR CURIOSITY

## *Words about Curiosity from Those Who Have Gone Before You*

Possibility breeds curiosity. Without curiosity, you cannot travel your own path—you simply travel whatever path is most obviously laid out before you. Or perhaps you don't travel at all. Without curiosity, why would you bother? Traveling is hard.

Consider for a moment that before you were born, you knew essentially nothing of the world, beyond what you could sense from inside the womb. Since then, you've been piecing things together. Connecting dots. Spinning stories. Building models in your mind. You can't help it—you're built for it.

Humans don't simply see stars. They connect them into constellations and see stories in the shapes. Humans kick pebbles to see how they'll tumble. They shake trees to see what falls out.

Humans look into the eyes of another and wonder what it is like to be her.

Curiosity is already within you, Warrior, but it can be developed or left to wither. Curiosity feeds on itself. One good question prompts more questions—which are at least as valuable as answers. Given the opportunity, your innate curiosity will make the world into a delightful, endlessly expanding place, ripe with possibility, and sexy as the scent of the hunt.

Given the opportunity. The opportunity to do what?

To *tinker*. How does this work? How did things get to be that way? What else is like this? How do we know that? Poke, prod, disassemble and reassemble everything. As a way of life. Every object, every idea is a widget, a gizmo, a thingamajig to be figured out. Including yourself.

To *explore*. What's over the next hill? Around the next corner? In the depths of the forest? At the bottom of the sea? In the corners of my mind? In the daily bustle of a different culture? Inside that dusty book? Just a mouse-click away? The actual finding is less important than honoring the impulse to seek.

To *test*. Humans construct all sorts of hypotheses about how things work, how things are, how things got to be. Some of those ideas seem to work; they explain what has happened and predict what will happen. Other hypotheses may not explain or predict so well, but we may find other uses for them: Quelling fears. Maintaining advantages. Delaying the expenditure of energy and money. Preserving a sense of worth. In the end, though, if the idea fails to explain and predict, it's a dead end. So, test ideas—your own and those of others. Use only two measures: how well they explain, how well they predict. All other measures are vanity.

Finally, a word on fear. Fear may not be the opposite of curiosity, but it is certainly curiosity's enemy. Fear animates machinery in your mind that disrupts the action of the delighted tinkerer, the fascinated seeker, the clear-eyed observer. Learn to sense when you are under the sway of fear. Notice how different you feel than when you are entranced by something new, immersed in figuring it out. You may notice that fear bends your thoughts towards judgment, towards conclusions about whether something is good or bad. And you may notice that, when curious, such judgments seem irrelevant. You're far less interested in *Whether* something will work, and far more interested in *How*.

We wish you curiosity, Warrior. That you may truly make your path your own.

*The Naked Truth*
with Eva Nogales, Ph.D.,
Professor of Biochemistry and
Molecular Biology, University
of California, Berkeley;
Investigator, Howard Hughes
Medical Institute; Senior Faculty
Scientist, Lawrence Berkeley
National Laboratory

Photo courtesy of Eva Nogales

Us: Hi Eva, Thanks for being part of our project!

E: It is my pleasure!

Us: Please tell us a little about yourself.

E: My parents were raised in post-Civil War Spain, and for ten years I myself lived under an extreme right-wing dictatorship. Then I lived through the coming of democracy, years that were very exciting. I very much enjoyed high school and was absolutely blessed with three spectacular female teachers in math, physics and biology. They really served as role models for me, and really made me appreciate how mathematics could explain physical phenomena. After considering going into medicine, I decided to go into physics—as far away from patients as I could!

I studied physics in Madrid, and then went to England to do my Ph.D. This was a very brave step for me, [taken] at a time when it was not common for people to leave Spain and go abroad for anything like that. That experience was very enriching and very humbling, because I had to learn biology and I was not at a university campus. I was at a national laboratory in the middle of nowhere. I basically tried to learn biology and biochemistry on my own, from primary literature in most cases. Then, I got incredibly lucky.

I was looking for post-docs, and my husband, who was my boyfriend at the time, was offered a position at Berkeley. I came by just looking for opportunities and I met Ken Downing, who was looking for post-docs to work on the structure of tubulin using the technique of electron crystallography, a discipline of cryo-electron microscopy (cryo-EM) that uses two-dimensional crystals. Tubulin is a protein that makes possible such vital life processes as cell division and the movement of materials within cells.

151

He took me into his lab in spite of the fact that I had not achieved a lot during my Ph.D. I like to joke that I would never make it today into my own lab. But Ken saw something in me, and I did have some experience in cryo-EM at a time when it was not very well known. My post-doc was hard. It was the type of project that makes you or breaks you. I had very bad times, there were tears, there was self-doubt, but the one thing I didn't lack was focus. I just kept going, and eventually it did work out. I obtained the structure of tubulin. That opened many doors for me.

I got a faculty position at Berkeley. Two years later I got selected as a Howard Hughes investigator. It's been a wonderful ride ever since. I work on structural biology, studying molecular mechanisms of important macromolecules in cellular function using cryo-EM. I work with a wonderful team of young men and women, students and post-docs. Meeting with them and discussing science with them is the best part of my day, which has many different parts. I love being in science and being in academia.

Us: Successful people often get the "what is your greatest advice" question, and we're going to ask it too. What is you best advice for young women?

E: My advice is that, whatever it is that they do, it has to feel good. It cannot be just a rational decision that you make but that leaves you with a knot in your stomach. Especially concerning science, it has to be that you really love the process . . . that you are going to have the strength to go through the ups and downs. Science is not for the weak of heart. Not everybody has to do science in the same way or at the same level, but everybody, no matter how successful they are, has to go through critical moments when things were not working, when you didn't know what the next step was or which way to turn. There has to be some joy that underlies the whole process, which keeps you going through the valleys so that you can eventually climb up the hill and be on top. I think it can't be "I think it's a good thing for the planet" or "I have to save humanity" or "that's what my parents want." It has to be that you really love it. Because, if you are doing cutting-edge, state-of-the-art research, you are at the frontier of knowledge and things are going to fail. You have to have something that motivates you and keeps you going.

Another thing is that you never do science alone. Not anymore. Maybe it was done that way in the past. Science—and it's a wonderful thing—is a team effort. There is nothing like surrounding yourself with lab members, from your mentor to your peers, with whom you are happy just sharing every day. Whom you trust as scientists and human beings, and you are just lucky to be with. It is much better to share those ups and downs with people that you like. Choose your team very carefully. That's super important.

Us: What do wish you had known earlier in your life that would have made your journey easier?

E: I wish that I had started reading something beyond my textbooks a little bit earlier on, to give me some breadth, a sense of looking beyond, toward that frontier of knowledge. Even though it may have been scary, because I may not have been able to understand everything. I wish that had been true, especially during my later days in high school and my earlier days in college.

My wish for what I had known later on is a bit different. When I go to give seminars at different campuses, I often have lunch with young women scientists. I often get asked how I am able to live the academic, scientific life, and also have a family life, children and all the rest? I would be lying if I didn't tell you: it's not a trivial challenge. Neither being a parent nor being a scientist are easy things. They're both very challenging and when you combine the two, well, it's challenging to the power of two. But, on the other hand, they are a beautiful complement. In principle, it has to be your choice, and I have known many women who have dealt with both beautifully. It can be done.

Photo courtesy of Eva Nogales

There are more and more ways that institutions are helping women, and men also, with parenting and the process of tenure, for example. They are taking steps to facilitate that, by giving you some teaching relief, delaying the time of your tenure process . . . I think those are good things and we should take advantage of them. We should not feel that there is something extra that we need to prove. Then we miss those critical years that happen during the graduate student, post-doc, and early tenure years, when most people will be considering having children and actually having them and not spending enough time with them. This I regret. I wish I had spent more time with my kids when they were little. . . .In 2000 they decided to grant Howard Hughes to very young assistant professors, and I felt under the double pressure of tenure and renewing my Howard Hughes. I was just working too hard. I could do it because I had a very supportive husband who was also a scientist, who understood what it took, and we managed. But I have a little bit of regret now that my kids are teenagers. My oldest one has gone to college and my memories of the two of them are a blur. It was such a rush. There is a way of making science and family compatible, and your kids are only going to be young once, so take advantage and find a happy equilibrium. Any opportunity that is given to you, legally or institutionally, just use it.

Us: What do you feel are the biggest obstacles that young women today have to face?

E: I think that there may be some external obstacles, certain perceptions, in many cases unconscious biases. I honestly believe that science and academia are more progressive, more advanced than other areas of society concerning matters of equality between genders. But still, from time to time, there could be characters who are a little more patronizing to women. Or who sometimes give women a kind of treatment that may make them uncomfortable.

I honestly have experienced very little of that. But it's also true that I grew up in a country where we had to get thicker skins. It's important that, if you find any discrimination or notice you've been treated in a way that is uncomfortable, you speak up. Not just for you, but for other women. I also think that we should build our own self-confidence . . . that we recognize, when acts like those occur, it's not about us. It's about others having problems and having issues and having to adapt. We should concentrate more on building self-esteem and building inner strength. But do it in a gentle manner, so that when we have self-doubt we don't beat ourselves up. That we consider it as part of a process that allows us to grow.

It is very important that you find groups of support. Your peers, but also mentors, women who have gone through the process that you may be going through at the time. They can give you perspective. I can assure you that when you talk to them, they will tell you "I have gone through that." There will be moments of self-doubt, it happens to everybody, but as women we might be a little bit more self-critical. There may be moments when you feel you've been treated a bit differently. Just be firm. Stand up. But move on.

Us: What important character traits came most naturally to you, and which do you think took the longest to develop?

E: I am naturally curious. I like to know. I like to investigate. I have a sense of wonder for discovery. I can put a lot of passion into what I do. I have energy to spare. Those things come very naturally to me. There are others that do not. I wouldn't even say that the others took me a long time to develop . . . I can't really say that I've reached a point where I can say I've got them, even now. One such thing is patience. I am very impatient, and that is not a good trait. Sometimes it comes through as being a little aggressive, or when I really let down people who need more time, who need to think about things more slowly. I think I need more gentleness and more patience dealing with issues, dealing with people, dealing with life. So I am still learning. The other thing that comes more slowly to me is perspective. You gain perspective with age. To have a broader view and be able to see whatever problem you are tackling in a much larger context, it always makes those problems seem smaller. Sometimes I can be just too overwhelmed.

Us: Growing up, what influences constrained you the most?

E: I didn't feel constrained, though I can give you examples of what things were like in Spain—just ten years into democracy—that will blow your mind. Neither of my parents actually finished middle school. They were brought up in a post-civil war period, when kids had to start working at the age of twelve, just to earn a living and to have food on the table. But they were absolutely obsessed with the education of their children. The number one priority in their lives was that my brother and me were going to go to school, were going to go to university, were going to get degrees, were going to be not only white-collar workers who earned a better salary than them, but people who were cultured, were educated, and were knowledgeable. For them, there was no difference between my brother and me. We both had the same potential. When I graduated high school, the three top students in my graduating class were women. One went into medicine and became a doctor. Another one was me, and I became a scientist. The third didn't go to college. She didn't go to college because her father didn't allow her to do it. And that was because she had an elder brother who, academically, was very bad, and did not make it into college. If the brother did not study in college, the father would not permit that the daughter go to college. Unbelievable! Inconceivable! Her teachers pleaded with her family and her father, yet her father would not allow it. That's why I really appreciate my parents, because they were free from that kind of perspective that otherwise was so rooted in other people.

Us: How do you know when you are on track, centered, and moving along your best path?

E: When people around me are happy, they're joyful, smiling. They are interacting with me in a way that is constructive. When I can be truthful to others, and others feel compelled to be truthful to me and communication is established, I think things are going well. One sign that there is something wrong is when you can no longer talk about what bothers you with the right people. The people who are involved, or the people who could help you, or the people that could advise you. If you get to that situation, where you have an issue that you can no longer express and find someone that you can confide in, it's a problem. You have to realize that something has to change. I don't always have all the answers of what to do. Sometimes you just have to force yourself to do what's needed, and sometimes you just have to let things go. There are always going to be things that are stressful, but if we can find a friend or a colleague to talk to, we can overcome them. If we do not, it all becomes bottled up inside, and that's bad. It's really important not to isolate yourself.

Us: What is the hardest decision you made right?

E: A decision that I took that, at the time, seemed very simple, but then sticking to it was hard, was to leave Spain to go do my Ph.D. abroad. In Spain, you go to the university that is closest to your parents, and you keep living with your parents. Families there are very tight and, in fact, people do their Ph.D. in the same place they did their bachelors, and stay in the same town. They never go. I had never been anywhere or done anything without my parents. I was also very gregarious, and I had always lived in the same town, so by the time I left, at 23, I had friends I had known for 20 years. And then I went to a new place, with a completely different culture. I didn't speak the language, and a lot was expected of me straight away, and my family and friends were not there. I did not think it through when I made the decision. I really spent a number of months in tears and very lonely for a long time. I could have gone back. I could have given up, and I didn't. That was fantastic, because once I overcame that, I never felt more fulfilled in my life.

Us: What do you do, and what do you tell yourself, when you have moments of self-doubt?

E: Because I have been through so many periods of self-doubt that I got out of, I tell myself something that my assistant expresses very well. She puts in two ways. One, by saying, "put one foot in front of the other." The other way, which I find very funny, is to say "Keep v and v." Vertical and ventilating! I know I will get out of it, if I just keep going. I concentrate on taking little steps, making it through the next hour, the next day, in a way that is not going to harm me or anyone else. We know that self-doubt is going to happen periodically, because we are doing things that are really difficult. You have the right to feel self-doubt. It really helps if you have someone to talk to. You can go to someone who you think "Oh, she's so great, she's always so upbeat. She's so successful." And she'll tell you, "Oh, I'm going through such a hard period, I really don't know what to do." And you think, "Ohhh, she's feeling just like me!" and we come out of it. We eventually overcome it and keep going. This is part of life. Part of what makes us more sympathetic toward others. Remember that you are not alone. Everybody goes through periods of self-doubt.

Us: To which of your own values do you attribute your success?

E: I am very persistent. In some cases, I have to admit, I was so persistent that I didn't consider, well, if this is not working out, why don't I do something else? It has to work. It has to work. It has to work. I am pretty good with analytical thinking. So I have that kind of intelligence. There are other kinds that I don't have. I have poor memory. It is terrible, because I have to relearn many things. But I can think very fast on my feet.

I wouldn't say that I am incredibly emotionally intelligent, but I can empathize with people. Sometimes I'm too distracted, but once I focus, I can engage with the person across from me. I can be truthful and engage on a level so that they feel comfortable working with me, talking to me and establishing a connection that helps us both.

Us: How much of your success derives from your own values and actions as opposed to external factors?

E: Luck is important. From time to time, chances are going to come your way and, if you have the talent to realize the opportunity, you jump on it. I have been very lucky. In a number of key situations, I have been in the right place at the right time. Luck and fortune favor those who are prepared. You just have to be alert.

Us: What else about you do you think young women would want to know?

E: One thing I haven't mentioned, and maybe that is because I haven't decided whether it is a positive or a negative, is that I can be kind of fearless. I don't mean I don't feel fear. I get super scared, but I still go through. There are moments where something is scary, but I feel it needs to be done. There is danger, maybe physical danger, maybe professional danger, but if it is my duty or there is a lot to gain, I just go and do it! There are many people who cannot do that. I don't know if it's foolishness, a sense of responsibility or a sense of fate, a sense that *I have to do this!* This has happened to me many times and it has been quite determining in my life. I'm telling you this, of course, only because I haven't yet fallen into the abyss. If I had fallen, I wouldn't be telling you my story. I can do courageous things.

# CHOOSE YOUR CURIOUS ADVENTURE!

## *Walkabout 1:*
### DEEP LISTENING INTERVIEW

Deep listening means we are listening with our full presence. Even when we hear something that we disagree with, when we bring compassion to the effort, we manage our feelings so that the other person has an opportunity to be completely heard. When we sit with curiosity and compassion for someone else, we learn volumes about the other and ourselves.

Select someone in your life you'd like to interview. She or he could be a teacher, family member, friend, or someone you'd like to get to know better. You can let them know this is part of your Wanderlust Warrior Project, if you wish, or you can keep it informal.

Prepare for the interview by thinking of questions beforehand. Make it a well-rounded interview by focusing on many areas of the person's life. Come up with something you want to know about their:

- Childhood
- Education
- Family life
- Career aspirations
- Life changing moments
- Social life
- Passions
- Beliefs
- Heroes
- Life challenges

Formulate your own questions in each area, and feel free to go beyond these written prompts. Come to the interview with your questions written down. Set an intention to listen deeply and picture in your mind what it looks like when you are listening with your full attention.

During the interview, as you listen to their responses, try to bring both concentration and curiosity to the conversation. What do you notice about this human being, sitting in front of you, and what are you learning about yourself as you practice the art of deep listening? How can you bring this skill with you in other areas of your life?

# WALKABOUT 2:
## KNOW THYSELF

We are constantly getting messages from our culture, schools, friends, churches, and families about who we are (or who we should be). Being susceptible to these messages is only human.

Take a moment and reflect on what you have accepted about what your world is telling you to be, for better or worse.

# THE MESSAGE

| | IS IT IN MY BEST INTEREST TO ACCEPT OR CHALLENGE THE MESSAGE? | WHAT CAN I SAY OR DO TO CHALLENGE THE MESSAGE? |
|---|---|---|
| PARENTS | | |
| SIBLINGS | | |
| FRIENDS | | |
| ROMANTIC PARTNERS | | |
| EXTENDED FAMILY | | |
| SCHOOL | | |
| TEACHERS | | |
| WORK | | |
| RELIGION / SPIRITUALITY | | |
| MOVIES / T.V. | | |

159

# THE MESSAGE

**IS IT IN MY BEST INTEREST TO ACCEPT OR CHALLENGE THE MESSAGE?**

**WHAT CAN I SAY OR DO TO CHALLENGE THE MESSAGE?**

MUSIC

SOCIAL MEDIA

ADVERTISING

FASHION

GOVERNMENT

NEIGHBORHOOD / COMMUNITY

EARTH

CULTURE

OTHER

160

# WALKABOUT 3:
## THE THREE BRAINS

Did you know we have more than one internal compass to turn to for intelligent guidance? That's why we hear things like, "Follow your heart," or "Trust your gut."

Our brain, our heart, and our gut work together to provide us helpful information. When we remember to tune into our three "brains," they can tell us things that we're typically too distracted to notice.

Call to mind an area of your life that stresses you out (but please don't think of the most stressful thing, just a typical stressor like running late, not getting a reply to your text, etc.) Close your eyes and focus on that stressor for a moment.

What do you notice about your thoughts when you are focused on the stressor? Watch the thoughts without judging them.

Bring your inner gaze to your heart. What is happening with your heart when you are connected to stress? Simply notice.

Next, bring your attention to your gut. What is it doing when you are connected to a stressful situation?

Take three conscious, intentional breaths.

With your eyes still closed, bring to mind something in your life that brings you peace or happiness (it could be music, your pet, a simple act of kindness). Allow yourself a full minute to imagine this pleasant situation.

Watch what happens to your mind as you focus on this picture of peace or happiness. Watch it without making internal comments.

Take a breath and bring your focus to your heart. What does the heart do as you tune into the pleasant experience? Be there for a full minute with your heart.

Next, drop your inner gaze down to the gut. As you linger on the positive, what does the gut do?

To close this exercise, with your eyes still closed, bring the palms of your hands together. Begin to rub them against each other, to generate warmth. Once your hands feel warm, bring your palms to your forehead, acknowledging and bringing kind attention to the brain. Sit for a few seconds and offer up words of thanks or encouragement to the brain. Next, place the palms of the hands on your heart. Offer words of acknowledgement to the heart. Finally, bring the palms of the hands to your belly. Smile to your belly and offer any closing words of gratitude.

What does tuning into the three brains do for
you? How can doing a self-check like this serve
you in difficult or happy times?

*Your Private Place for Notes or Doodles*

Photo credit: Danielle Trina Photography

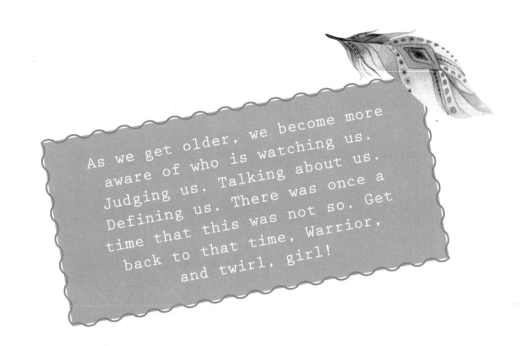

As we get older, we become more aware of who is watching us. Judging us. Talking about us. Defining us. There was once a time that this was not so. Get back to that time, Warrior, and twirl, girl!

# THE END OR THE BEGINNING?

Where are we now? Are we at the beginning of something new, Warrior? Or are we at the end of a chapter in your life? You might feel like you want to change some things about how you live—and that's wonderful! Perhaps you feel as if you are ending a cycle you've been living. Entering into a new, more mature way of seeing the world, and leaving your childhood—and that's great too. But the truth is, Young Warrior, that you're not ending or starting anything. You've always been here. You've been traveling your path since you were born. You will continue to travel the path until you die. There's no arrival. You do not one day end up where you strived to be and stay there. Your beautiful, unique life continues to unfold itself to you with each passing day, year, decade. You learn. You grow. You continuously blossom, and blossom, and blossom into the whole of you.

Please don't be in a rush to get somewhere. Certainly, being ambitious, excited, and striving to meet your goals is admirable. But please don't go too fast on your journey. No matter what whispers from others are filling your ears. You risk missing the fullness of life and what makes for a life well-lived. The small observations, the acknowledgement of the extraordinary, the curiosity of life's strangeness—life is made of these seemingly insignificant things. But they are not insignificant at all, Warrior. Stitched together, the small wonders make a life worth living. The challenge is in slowing down enough to actually see, touch, feel, and witness the beauty of this one, magical life you have been given. When we rush too fast into our future, we will always miss the miracles all around us. And, yes, there will be days of rushing. There may even be weeks or years of hurrying around, attempting to achieve some arbitrary goal which, in the end, will seem unworthy of that rush. But you will do it anyway. We all have. Knowing when to slow it all down, center yourself, and come back to that pure place where you feel whole and free, where the noise of the world ceases and you know, really know, that you were made perfect and imperfect from the beginning . . . that's what makes you a Wanderlust Warrior, and not simply a wanderer.

Please do not compare your journey with that of others on their own unique paths. Each life is different, deeply experienced only by the person living it. There are no steadfast rules for what your path should look like. In fact, the lack of rules is what makes for a glorious life experience. Paths and tracks and roads and journeys that swirl around, intersect, go in and out and all around, bumping into, bumping out of, moving away from, moving toward. Life is a tapestry of beautiful movement. It is a song, a piece of art, a dance. When you can see each individual's dance of life, and appreciate theirs as much as yours, you will see how we all fit together. We are, each of us, alone and together, dancing our way home.

There is no end and no beginning. All there is, is now. Where you are at this moment. Your next choice is yours to make. It will always be so. Your next step can hold all the greatness you ever imagined. Your very next step can change the direction of your magnificent life. Choose carefully, Warrior. And use the tools you have been given.

Remember, you have been given gifts early in your journey. You have been given the *strength* to carry your own pack and lend a hand to others. You understand being *independent*, walking alone when your path requires it. You are building *confidence* to believe in your own ability and face your challenges head on. You will walk with *kindness*, with empathy and an open heart. You will rely on your *intelligence* to see through the sparkling distractions all around you. Your *wisdom* will grasp the lessons of the stories you encounter along the trail of your life. You continue your voyage with *bravery*, so you can march forward with fear as your companion. Your *honesty* will always be with you, so you can never shrink away from the raw reality that is within you and all around you. And finally, with *curiosity* as a torch to light your adventure, you will uncover your own truth, in your own time, in your own way.

Remember, your Warrior Tribe will want so much for you, but we know there is very little that we can control. There is only one thing that we promise you: we will be here. We are right behind you. We are on the sides of you. We always will be. But we are not in front of you. We do not block you. Now, run!

NOT THE END.
NOT THE BEGINNING.